FXCK THEM

Also by **WALLO267**

The Mind of Wallo

Armed with Good Intentions

Social Media Made Me Do It

3 Buckets

FXCK THEM

WALLO267

NANNY'S HOUSE PUBLISHING

Pennsauken, New Jersey

Cover Design: Kamera Krew LLC
Interior Design: Jessica Angerstein
Mananging Company: IV MGMT, LLC

Cataloging-in-Publication Data is on file with the Library of Congress.

Paperback ISBN: 979-8-9945002-6-2
ebook ISBN: 979-8-9945002-7-9

1 2 3 4 5 6 7 8 9 10
First edition, February 2026

This book is for the version of you that finally got tired of being convenient. For the one who learned that peace built on silence is just self-betrayal.

For the one who over-explained, over-gave, and waited on permission from people who never planned to give it. For you, if choosing yourself made people uncomfortable.

If walking away cost you access, approval, or relationships you were never meant to keep. If staying was slowly killing you and you chose to leave anyway. This book is not here to heal you.

It is here to remind you that you allowed too much—and that stops now. Read it when you're done asking. Read it when you're ready to choose yourself without apology.

Contents

Chapter 1: FXCK THEM is a decision, not a feeling................1

Chapter 2: Most people are background noise 9

Chapter 3: Opinions multiply when you start moving..........17

Chapter 4: You were never supposed to be
this accessible... 25

Chapter 5: Everyone cannot come with you 33

Chapter 6: Caring too much is a form of self-neglect 41

Chapter 7: People love you based on the version
that benefits them 49

Chapter 8: You are not required to carry other
people's comfort 57

Chapter 9: Explaining yourself is a trap................................ 65

Chapter 10: They call it humble because it keeps
you manageable... 73

Chapter 11: FXCK THEM does not mean you are cold,
it means you are clear 81

Chapter 12: The real fear is not failure, it is disappointing
people who expect you to stay the same 89

Chapter 13: Distance reveals everything................................97

Chapter 14: Respect is felt before it is spoken.................... 105

Chapter 15: You are allowed to choose yourself repeatedly, even when people get tired of it 113

Chapter 16: Being liked is not a life goal................................. 121

Chapter 17: The day you stop seeking permission............. 129

Chapter 18: Let them misunderstand you 137

Chapter 19: Your life will get quieter, and that is the point 145

Chapter 20: FXCK THEM is how you finally live................. 151

Chapter 21: Comfort is the most expensive drug you'll ever take 157

Chapter 22: Discipline is real..165

Chapter 23: Nobody is coming to save you 175

Chapter 24: You will outgrow this version of yourself too 183

Chapter 25: Pressure is proof you are leveling up............... 191

Chapter 26: Stop reading. Start moving............................... 199

Final Truth 205

About the Author 209

Keep in touch with WALLO267.. 211

FXCK THEM IS NOT SOMETHING YOU FEEL.

IT IS SOMETHING YOU DECIDE.

FXCK THEM is a decision, not a feeling

If you picked up this book looking for comfort, you already started wrong. This is not therapy. This is not encouragement. This is not somebody holding your hand and telling you it will be okay. This is a mirror, and you are not going to like what you see at first.

Most people think FXCK THEM is an emotion. They think it is anger. They think it is a reaction. They think it is something you say when you are hurt, embarrassed, rejected, or fed up. That is why most people never actually live it. They only say it on bad days. They only say it after they have already been disrespected. They only say it when the damage is already done. That is a weakness.

FXCK THEM is not something you feel. It is something you decide. Feelings change. Decisions don't, unless you fold. And most of you fold daily. You fold when you overexplain. You fold when you delay. You fold when you choose comfort over truth. You fold when you keep people around who drain you because you are scared of what life looks like without them.

You say you are tired. You say you are stuck. You say you do not know what to do next. That is a lie. You know exactly what to do. You just do not want the consequences that come with finally doing it. You want change without friction. Growth without discomfort. Freedom without loss. That is not how life works, and deep down you know it.

You do not lack motivation. You lack courage. You are not confused. You are avoiding. You are not waiting on timing. You are waiting on permission.

FXCK THEM starts when you stop pretending your hesitation is noble. It is not loyalty. It is fear. It is not patience. It is cowardice dressed up as maturity. It is not being considerate. It is self-abandonment.

Every day you wake up and give people a vote in your life who have done nothing to earn it. People who are not building. People who are not disciplined. People who are not consistent. People who would not last one week under the pressure you silently carry. Yet you let their opinions slow you down. You let their reactions shape your decisions. You let their comfort dictate your truth. That is insanity.

You were not put on this planet to manage other people's feelings. You were not designed to be this accessible. You were not meant to check in with everyone before you made a move. Somewhere along the way, you were trained to believe that being liked is the same as being respected. It is not. Liked people get used. Respected people get left alone.

Read that again slowly.

The reason this book has to be aggressive is because your situation is not gentle. Your life is passing you in real time while you sit around negotiating with people who do not even understand the weight of your potential. Time is moving whether you make a decision or not. Comfort is expensive, and you pay for it over years.

Most people never choose FXCK THEM. They wait until life forces it. They wait until betrayal humiliates them. They wait until exhaustion breaks them. They wait until resentment poisons them. Then they finally snap and call it growth. That is not growth. That is damage control. This book is about choosing yourself before life embarrasses you into it.

FXCK THEM means you stop asking how everyone will feel and start asking where your life is actually going. It means you stop explaining your vision to people who benefit from you staying small. It means you stop watering yourself down to be digestible to people who were never meant to consume your future.

And let me be clear. This does not make you cruel. It makes you honest. It does not make you selfish. It makes you responsible. It does not make you cold. It makes you focused.

People will call you different when you change. They will say you switched up. They will say you think you are better. They will say you forgot where you came from. None of that matters. What they are really saying is you stopped being convenient.

The moment you decide FXCK THEM, you will feel guilt. That guilt is not morality. It is conditioning. You were trained to put yourself last and call it character. You were trained to sacrifice your direction to keep peace, but that never lasts. You were trained to believe that saying no requires an explanation. It does not.

You do not need to convince anyone. You do not need to be understood. You do not need permission. You need movement.

Understand this right now. People will survive your absence. They always do. What has not survived is your potential every time you choose them over yourself. That is the real tragedy.

This chapter is not here to hype you up. It is here to strip excuses. If you cannot decide FXCK THEM in your mind, you will never live it in your actions. Everything else in this book depends on this moment. Not later. Not after one more conversation. Not after one more sign. Now.

Because waiting is still a decision. And it is the one that keeps you exactly where you are.

Chapter 1

ACTION PLAN FOR CHANGE

1. Write down the names of three people whose opinions currently influence your decisions more than your own values. Do not justify it. Just write the names.

   _____

   _____

   _____

2. Identify one decision you have been delaying because of how those people might react. Be specific. No general statements.

3. Decide today whether you are willing to accept their temporary discomfort in exchange for your

long-term peace. If the answer is no, admit that you are choosing comfort over growth.

4. For the next seven days, stop explaining yourself. Make decisions and let them stand without defense or apology.

5. Read this chapter again after one week and notice how different it hits once you stop pretending your hesitation is something other than fear.

When you are ready, turn the page. If not, close the book. Either way, the decision is yours now.

MOST PEOPLE ARE BACKGROUND NOISE, NOT DIRECTION.

Most people are background noise

You give too much meaning to people who barely understand their own lives.

That sentence alone will make some of you uncomfortable because you have built your identity around being seen, heard, validated, and acknowledged by people who are not qualified to understand you. You listen to everybody. You absorb opinions like they are facts. You let comments linger in your mind longer than your own goals. That is not awareness. That is weakness disguised as openness.

Most people are background noise. Not villains. Not enemies. Not evil. Just irrelevant to the direction of your life.

And the reason that truth is hard to accept is because you have been trained to believe that proximity equals importance. That because someone is around you, they deserve a say. Because they have a history with you, they deserve influence. Because they share blood, a workplace, a neighborhood, or a timeline, they automatically get a vote.

That is a lie that keeps people stuck.

Familiarity does not equal wisdom. Loud does not equal right. Longevity does not equal alignment. And opinions do not become valuable just because they are repeated often.

The average person you listen to has no plan. No discipline. No long-term vision. No control over their own impulses. They react to life instead of directing it. They complain instead of building. They cope instead of changing. Yet you let their perspective slow your momentum.

That should bother you.

You do not need to hear everyone. You need to hear the right things. And most of what surrounds you daily is not insight. It is noise. It is people projecting their limitations, fears, regrets, and unrealized dreams onto you because watching you move forces them to confront their own inaction.

So they comment. They question. They warn. They doubt. They joke. They criticize. They disguise insecurity as concern and hesitation as wisdom.

And you fall for it because part of you is still looking for approval from the room instead of clarity from yourself.

Background noise is dangerous because it sounds normal. It sounds familiar. It blends in. It does not announce itself as sabotage. It shows up as casual conversation, jokes, warnings, advice, opinions, and reactions that feel harmless individually but destructive collectively.

One voice does not derail you. Twenty do.

That is why your mind feels crowded. That is why you feel overwhelmed. That is why you second-guess decisions you already knew were right. That is why you feel drained after nonproductive conversations. You are mentally over-exposed.

Not every thought deserves your attention. Not every opinion deserves your consideration. Not every voice deserves space in your head. You have mistaken access for entitlement.

People who are background noise should not get front row seating in your life.

Here is the hard part. Most of the noise comes from people you care about. Friends, family, coworkers, partners, people who love you but do not understand you. People who want the best for you, as long as it does not disrupt the version of you they are comfortable with.

That is why detachment feels cruel at first. You think ignoring noise means ignoring people. It does not. It means prioritizing your direction over their commentary.

You do not owe everyone your attention. Attention is currency. And you are broke because you give it away freely.

The most successful people are not smarter than you. They are quieter. They know when to listen and when to disengage. They know that not every thought needs a response. They know that silence is not weakness. It is filtration.

You are allowed to let people talk without waiting for their words to settle. You are allowed to hear without absorbing. You are allowed to observe without engaging. That is not arrogance. That is self-preservation.

Most people speak from emotion, not intention. They speak from fear, not experience. They speak from comfort, not courage. And if you let that guide you, you will live a very safe, very average life that feels busy but goes nowhere.

Pay attention to who gets quiet when you talk about growth. Who jokes when you talk about discipline? Who doubts when you talk about change? That silence and those jokes are not accidental. They are information.

Not everyone is meant to walk with you. Some people are just meant to pass by. Others are meant to stay in the background. And a few are meant to lead the way.

Your job is to know the difference.

Right now, you are treating background noise like direction. That is why you feel lost. That is why you keep restarting. That is why every step forward feels heavy. You are carrying too many voices that were never meant to be yours.

Clarity comes when the noise fades.

And the noise only fades when you stop giving it power.

Chapter 2

ACTION PLAN FOR CHANGE

1. For the next five days, observe how many opinions you consume daily through conversations, social media, and casual commentary. Do not react. Just notice.

2. Identify which voices consistently leave you feeling doubtful, drained, or hesitant. Write them down without judgment.

3. Decide which opinions are earned through experience, results, and alignment, and which are just noise. Be honest, even if it hurts.

4. Reduce exposure. Less conversation, less scrolling, less explaining. Protect your mental space like it matters because it does.

5. Replace noise with intention. Read, listen, and learn only from sources that challenge you to move, not shrink.

When you quiet the background, your direction gets louder.

PROGRESS CREATES NOISE. STAGNATION CREATES SILENCE.

Opinions multiply when you start moving

Nobody had much to say when you were standing still.

Sit with that.

When you were quiet, average, and predictable—when you blended in and stayed manageable—nobody had advice. When you talked about ideas but never acted on them, when your dreams stayed small enough to be ignored, nobody had concerns or warnings. Nobody had an opinion worth voicing.

The moment you start moving, everything changes.

All of a sudden, everybody has something to say: a story, a warning, someone who tried that. Everybody sees the risk and wants to pull you aside for a talk, reminding you to be careful, to be realistic, to slow down, to think about how this looks.

That is not a coincidence. That is exposure.

Movement threatens comfort. Especially the comfort of people who are watching you do what they talked themselves out of doing.

Opinions multiply when you start moving because progress forces comparison. And comparison makes insecure people uncomfortable. Your action highlights their inaction, your discipline exposes their excuses, and your growth reminds them of the version of themselves they abandoned. Instead of confronting that truth, they aim it at you.

So they talk.

They do not say I am scared, I waited too long, I quit on myself. Instead, they say you are changing, you are doing too much, you are moving too fast. They say you need to relax, do not forget where you came from, and be humble. They ask why rush.

What they really mean is, please slow down, so I do not have to face what I did not do.

You need to understand this deeply. Opinions are not feedback. They are reactions. Reactions say more about the person reacting than the person being moved.

Progress creates noise. Stagnation creates silence. If nobody is talking about what you are doing, it is usually because you are not doing enough to disrupt anything. Silence feels safe, peaceful, even like approval, but it also means invisibility. It means you are not challenging anything or threatening the status quo, including your own.

Most people say they want change, but they want quiet change—change that does not attract attention, upset anyone, require confrontation, or cost relationships. That kind of change does not exist.

Every real move you make will offend someone.

Every boundary will confuse someone.

Every step forward will trigger commentary.

And if you let that stop you, then you were never committed to moving in the first place.

You need to stop interpreting increased opinions as a sign that that you are doing something wrong. It is usually a sign you are finally doing something right. The noise is proof of impact. The discomfort is evidence of momentum. The pushback is confirmation that you are no longer invisible.

The mistake you keep making is thinking that movement requires consensus. It does not. It requires conviction.

You keep slowing down to explain, pausing to reassure, justifying decisions that do not need justification. Every time you do that, you lose rhythm, confidence, and clarity.

Momentum dies when you stop to debate with people who are not going anywhere.

Here is a hard truth. People who are actively building do not have time to manage your choices. They are too busy managing their own. The loudest opinions almost always come from the least active people in the room.

Watch closely. The ones who are moving rarely comment. They nod. They observe. They respect the process. The ones who are stuck narrate everything.

So ask yourself this: Why are you listening to people who are not in motion, weighing opinions that come with no results, letting spectators coach your life?

You do not ask someone sitting in the stands how to run the play.

The reason opinions feel heavy right now is that you are still emotionally tied to being understood. You want people to get it. You want them to see your heart. You want them to understand your intention. That need will cost you everything if you let it. You are not required to be understood during growth. Understanding comes later. Sometimes much later. Sometimes never.

And that is okay.

You need to accept that moving forward means being misunderstood, that clarity is not immediate, that some people will mislabel you while others doubt you, and that a few will secretly hope you fail because it makes their own choices easier to live with. Let them.

Your job is not to manage narratives. Your job is to move.

Opinions will come whether you succeed or fail. If you fail, they will say you should have listened. If you succeed, they will say they always believed in you. Either way, the commentary exists. The only difference is where you end up. So choose movement.

Stop looking at opinions as obstacles. They are weather. They pass. You keep walking.

Stop reacting emotionally to every comment. Emotional reaction is still permission. Calm detachment is power.

The faster you move, the less time you have to listen. And that is the point.

Momentum is the greatest filter you have.

When you are moving with intention, the noise fades because it cannot keep up.

Chapter 3

ACTION PLAN FOR CHANGE

1. Identify one area of your life where increased opinions have recently appeared. Do not minimize it. Write it down.

2. Ask yourself honestly what triggered the noise: a decision, a boundary, a new habit, a risk. Movement always precedes commentary.

3. Stop explaining that decision immediately. No clarifying texts, no long conversations, no defending. Let the action stand on its own.

4. Commit to moving faster in that area for the next thirty days. Speed reduces doubt and silences unnecessary voices.

5. Each time an opinion surfaces, ask one question before reacting: Is this coming from someone actively doing what I want to do? If not, let it pass without response.

Noise is proof that you are moving. Keep going.

YOU OWE NOBODY IMMEDIATE ACCESS TO YOU.

You were never supposed to be this accessible

Your biggest mistake was mistaking availability for value.

At some point, you were taught that being reachable meant being respectful, that answering every call, responding to every message, explaining every decision, and being constantly present was a sign of maturity, kindness, or loyalty. You were trained to believe that distance was rude and boundaries were selfish, so you opened yourself up to everyone and called it character.

What you really did was remove all protection from your life.

You were never supposed to be this accessible. No human being was. Constant access was never part of healthy living; it is a modern trap disguised as connection. Technology did not just make communication easier. It erased distance, and distance used to protect people from each other.

Now everyone can reach you whenever they want, interrupting your thoughts, your focus, your momentum, your peace. Instead of guarding yourself, you answer because you do not want to be seen as difficult, ungrateful, or distant.

That is how people slowly lose themselves.

Accessibility creates entitlement. When people can reach you anytime, they start believing they deserve access at any time. They stop respecting your time, your energy, and your space, and you let it happen because you trained them to.

Every unanswered call makes you feel guilty. Every delayed reply feels like you are doing something wrong. Every moment of silence feels like tension. That is not connection. That is control.

You do not realize how much of your exhaustion comes from being constantly available. You are not tired because you are doing too much; you are tired because you are interruptible. Your mind never settles, your body never rests, and your focus never locks in. You are always on call for someone else's needs, questions, problems, or emotions.

That is not life. That is servitude.

You cannot build anything meaningful while being this accessible. You cannot think deeply when you are constantly interrupted. You cannot evolve while everyone has a direct line to your attention. Great things require isolation periods. Focus seasons. Distance from noise. That is not arrogance. That is a necessity.

People will tell you you changed when you become less accessible. They will say you are acting differently. They will say you disappeared. They will say you are too busy. What they really mean is you are no longer immediately available to them.

And that bothers people who benefited from your availability.

The truth is, access should be earned. Not granted by default. Proximity should not guarantee influence. And constant communication should not be confused with closeness.

You owe nobody immediate access to you.

Read that again until it settles.

You owe nobody instant replies, constant availability, explanations for needing space, or your attention simply because they want it.

The reason this feels wrong to you is that you were conditioned to believe your worth is tied to how needed you are.

You learned to feel valuable when people depended on you. When they called you. When they needed your advice, your presence, your reassurance. So you stayed available even when it cost you yourself.

That is how people become emotionally overdrawn.

You give and give and give until resentment builds, then you feel guilty for the resentment, then you give more to compensate. That cycle will destroy you quietly.

Being accessible is not the same as being supportive. Being distant is not the same as being uncaring. The difference is intention.

You can love people without being reachable at all times, care without carrying everyone, and support without sacrificing your direction.

The people who truly respect you will adjust. The ones who benefited from your availability will resist. That resistance is information.

Watch who gets offended when you create space, who demands explanations, who guilt-trips you, and who makes your boundary about them. Those reactions reveal who was feeding off your access instead of respecting your presence.

You do not need to announce boundaries; you need to enforce them. Announcements invite debate, while enforcement creates clarity.

You are not disappearing; you are prioritizing. You are not acting brand new; you are acting intentionally. You are not ignoring people; you are protecting your future.

The strongest shift you will ever make is becoming less available to people who are not aligned with where you are going. That single change will return energy you forgot you had. Clarity you thought you lost. Focus you thought was gone forever.

Accessibility is addictive because it makes you feel important. But the importance that drains you is not important. It is exploitation.

Your life will not change until your availability does.

Every time you choose not to respond immediately, you reclaim a piece of yourself. Every time you delay access, you regain control. Every time you create space, you create room for growth.

Silence is not neglect. It is design.

Distance is not punishment. It is protection.

And anyone who truly values you will understand that.

Chapter 4

ACTION PLAN FOR CHANGE

1. Identify who currently has unlimited access to you through calls, messages, drop-ins, or emotional dumping. This is about access, not affection. Write their names down.

2. Choose one boundary to implement immediately, such as delayed responses, scheduled availability, or limited conversation windows. Do not redesign your entire life. That's how boundaries fail.

3. Stop explaining why you need space, because explanations invite negotiation. Let your behavior speak. Boundaries aren't arguments to be won—they're conditions of engagement.

4. Use reclaimed time intentionally to read, plan, think, rest, and build. Do not fill the space with more noise. Guard this space fiercely at first. It's fragile.

5. Observe reactions without guilt. Respect reveals itself when access is limited. Let the reactions be data, not a verdict on your character.

Your life will open up the moment you stop being available to everyone.

GROWTH SEPARATES. PROGRESS ISOLATES. EVOLUTION COSTS RELATIONSHIPS.

Chapter 5

Everyone cannot come with you

This is the chapter most people avoid because it forces them to admit a truth they do not want to acknowledge. Everyone cannot come with you. Not because you are better. Not because you are special. Not because you think highly of yourself. But because growth changes terrain, not everyone is built to walk where you are going.

You keep trying to drag people into futures they did not prepare for. You keep slowing your pace to match people who are comfortable standing still. You keep explaining your vision to people who do not even have one of their own. Then you wonder why the journey feels heavy.

It is heavy because you are carrying people who were never meant to walk beside you.

FXCK THEM

Nobody tells you this early enough. Growth separates. Progress isolates. Evolution costs relationships. And pretending otherwise only delays the inevitable. You do not outgrow people because you want to. You outgrow them because staying the same would require betraying yourself.

You keep asking how to bring everyone along instead of asking who is actually aligned. You keep looking for ways to adjust your path so nobody feels left behind. You keep negotiating your direction so nobody feels abandoned. In the process, you abandon yourself daily and call it loyalty.

That loyalty is misplaced.

Some people are in your life for a season. Others for a lesson. A few for a lifetime. The mistake is treating everyone like they belong in all three categories. That confusion will ruin your momentum.

People like you when you are familiar. When you stay the version they understand. When your growth does not force them to reevaluate their own choices. The moment you shift, you disrupt the relationship dynamic. You are no longer predictable. You are no longer available in the same way. You are no longer manageable.

And that is when resistance shows up.

Not everyone will clap when you change. Some will question you, some will doubt you, some will joke, and some will guilt you. Some will pull you aside and remind you of who you used to be, as if that version was a requirement.

They are not trying to hurt you. They are trying to keep you where they are comfortable.

This is where most people fold. They mistake discomfort for betrayal. They confuse separation with disloyalty. They believe choosing themselves means hurting others. That belief keeps them stuck in rooms they have already outgrown. You are allowed to grow without dragging everyone with you. Read that slowly.

You are allowed to move forward even if people stay behind. You are allowed to change even if it makes others uncomfortable. You are allowed to choose your future even if it does not include everyone from your past.

The hardest part is accepting that some people cannot follow you because they do not want to. Others cannot follow because they lack the capacity. And some simply do not recognize you once you stop being convenient.

That is not your responsibility.

You are not obligated to sacrifice your evolution to preserve relationships that only work when you are small, not required to stay accessible to people who only value you when you are available, and not selfish for choosing alignment over attachment.

Attachment without alignment is a trap. The reason letting go feels painful is that you attach identity to proximity. You believe history should guarantee access. You believe shared memories should guarantee future presence. But memories do not build futures. Decisions do.

People who are meant to come with you will adjust, ask questions, learn, respect your boundaries, and support your growth even if it stretches them. People who are not meant to come will resist change and call it concern.

Pay attention to who supports your discipline and who only supports your comfort. That distinction matters more than words.

You do not need to announce departures, explain transitions, or have closure conversations with everyone. Movement creates its own separation. Distance happens naturally when alignment disappears. Trying to force togetherness only creates resentment. Letting go is not abandonment. It is acceptance.

You are not leaving people behind. You are answering a call they do not hear.

Every level of life requires a different version of you. And different versions of you require different environments. Some people belong to earlier chapters of your story. That does not make them bad. It makes them complete.

Dragging unfinished relationships into new seasons creates friction you do not need. It dilutes your focus. It pulls you backward emotionally, even while you move forward physically. You have to learn how to release without guilt.

You can love people and still create distance, appreciate history and still choose a different future, and be grateful and still move on. Growth does not ask for permission. It demands alignment.

The fear you feel is not about losing people. It is about facing who you become without them. It is about standing alone long enough to hear your own voice clearly. That silence scares people more than the company that drains them. But that silence is where clarity lives.

It's not about cutting everyone off. It's about not dragging people who are not walking. Stop pausing your life to wait on people who are comfortable where they are. Stop confusing shared pasts with shared futures.

Everyone cannot come with you. And the moment you accept that, your life gets lighter.

Chapter 5

ACTION PLAN FOR CHANGE

1. Write down the names of people you consistently slow down for emotionally, mentally, or physically.

   _____

   _____

   _____

2. Ask yourself one honest question for each name: Are they growing with me, or am I shrinking for them?

3. Identify one relationship where distance is necessary right now, not forever, but right now.

4. Create that distance without explanation through less access, less conversation, and less emotional labor.

5. Use the energy you reclaim to invest in your direction. Growth requires room. Make some.

Let go without anger. Move without guilt. The people meant to walk with you will keep pace.

CARING TOO MUCH IS NOT KINDNESS.

IT IS AVOIDANCE.

Caring too much is a form of self-neglect

You were taught to care before you were taught to choose yourself. That lesson cost you more than you realize.

Somewhere early on, you learned that being considerate meant being available, that being a good person meant being understanding, and that caring deeply meant absorbing other people's emotions, carrying their stress, softening your truth, and delaying your needs. You were praised for being thoughtful, patient, and understanding. Nobody told you that, taken too far, those traits turn into self-neglect.

And now look at you.

You are emotionally exhausted but still showing up for everyone, drained but still listening, and overwhelmed but still saying it is fine. You keep confusing empathy with obligation, and it is killing your momentum quietly.

Caring too much is not kindness. It is avoidance.

It is avoiding conflict, disappointment, being seen as self-ish, and the discomfort that comes with choosing yourself. So instead, you over-care, over-listen, over-extend, over-explain, and over-accommodate. And you under-live.

You call it being mature. It is not. It is self abandonment.

There is a difference between compassion and self-erasure. Compassion acknowledges others without sacrificing yourself. Self-erasure puts everyone else first and calls it love. One builds a connection. The other builds resentment.

You feel that resentment growing, and then you feel guilty for it. So you care more to compensate. That cycle never ends unless you deliberately interrupt it.

People take what you offer. They rarely stop you. They rarely say you have done enough. They rarely tell you to rest. They will gladly let you burn yourself out while they remain comfortable. Not because they are evil, but because you taught them it was allowed.

You trained people to expect access to your emotions, your time, your attention, and your patience. And now, when you try to pull back, it feels wrong to you even though it is right for you.

That is conditioning.

You do not owe everyone your emotional labor, your understanding, or your patience. And you definitely do not owe people your peace.

The hardest truth is this. Some people only feel supported when you are sacrificing yourself. They do not know how to exist in a relationship with you unless you are carrying more than your share. The moment you stop over-caring, they feel abandoned even though you are still present.

That is not your problem.

Caring without boundaries turns into control disguised as closeness. People get used to your emotional availability and confuse it with entitlement. They begin to expect you to show up no matter what, to listen no matter how tired you are, and to accommodate no matter the cost. When you finally say no, they act shocked, offended, or hurt.

They are not reacting to your behavior. They are reacting to the loss of their benefit.

You need to hear this clearly. Caring too much does not make you a better person. It makes you an exhausted one. And exhaustion does not lead to clarity. It leads to resentment, passive aggression, and emotional withdrawal.

That is why some of you feel numb. You are not cold. You are depleted.

You gave without limit, and now you have nothing left for yourself. You cannot build a future from that place.

The people who truly respect you will not demand self-sacrifice as proof of love. They will not need you to drain yourself to feel supported. They will adjust when you pull back. They will respect your boundaries even if it takes time.

The ones who do not will guilt you. They will remind you of everything you have done. They will accuse you of changing. They will frame your boundaries as betrayal. That reaction is information.

Caring less does not mean you stop loving. It means you start choosing. It means you decide who gets access and when. It means you stop being the emotional dumping ground for people who refuse to manage their own lives.

You are not responsible for regulating other people's feelings. That responsibility belongs to them. The moment you accept that your nervous system will finally get a break.

You have been living like a support system instead of a person, always steady, always available, always understanding, always absorbing. And now you wonder why nobody supports you the same way.

It is because you never required it.

Over-caring creates imbalance. And imbalance breeds resentment.

You cannot save everyone, carry everyone, or heal everyone. And trying to do so does not make you noble. It makes you distracted from your own life.

There is nothing honorable about neglecting yourself.

Real care has limits, structure, and includes you.

The moment you stop caring, you will feel uncomfortable. You will feel selfish. You will feel like you are doing something wrong. That feeling is withdrawal. You are detoxing from approval and emotional dependency.

Let it pass.

You will also feel lighter, clearer, more focused, and more present in your own life. That feeling is freedom.

You were never meant to care yourself into invisibility.

Care is a resource. Spend it intentionally.

Chapter 6

ACTION PLAN FOR CHANGE

1. Identify one situation where you consistently overcare at your own expense. Be specific and honest. Be specific. Name the person, the setting, and the pattern.

2. Decide on one boundary to implement immediately in that situation through less listening, less availability, and less emotional labor.

3. When guilt shows up, do not react to it. Sit with it. Guilt is not a command. Guilt is an emotion—not an instruction, not a moral failing, not a debt.

4. Redirect that energy toward yourself for one week to rest, plan, move, and build something that belongs to you.

5. Pay attention to who respects the shift and who resists it. Respect reveals alignment. Alignment shows up when your care for yourself doesn't threaten the relationship.

Caring less is not cruelty. It is survival.

PEOPLE LOVE THE VERSION OF YOU THAT MAKES THEIR LIFE EASIER.

People love you based on the version that benefits them

Most people do not love you unconditionally. They love the version of you that fits comfortably into their life.

That truth hurts because it exposes something you do not want to admit. A lot of the support you thought was love was actually convenience. A lot of the praise you received was conditional. A lot of the closeness you felt existed because you were predictable, manageable, and easy to deal with.

When you were available, they loved you.

When you were agreeable, they loved you.

When you stayed the same, they loved you.

The moment you change, the tone shifts.

Suddenly, you are different, distant, selfish, doing too much. Suddenly, you think you are better, that you forgot where you came from.

No. You stopped being useful to the version of them that relied on your consistency.

People get attached to the roles you play, not the person you are becoming. When you step out of that role, they feel threatened, confused, or abandoned. Not because you hurt them, but because you disrupted the arrangement.

Every relationship has an unspoken agreement. You behave a certain way. They benefit in a certain way. As long as that exchange stays intact, everything feels smooth. The moment you grow, the agreement breaks.

And broken agreements make people uncomfortable.

You were the listener, the fixer, the dependable one who stayed calm, showed up, never made waves, understood, and sacrificed. That version of you made other people's lives easier.

Of course, they loved that version. But that version cost you everything. When you decide to evolve, you stop performing that role, absorbing everyone else's needs, prioritizing their comfort, and being endlessly available. And suddenly, people say they do not recognize you anymore.

What they really mean is they cannot benefit from you the same way.

This is where people get confused. They think resistance means they are doing something wrong. They think push-back means they are being cruel. They think guilt means they should revert. That is how people trap themselves in outdated versions of their own lives.

You are not responsible for maintaining an identity that no longer fits you.

People who truly care about you will struggle with change, but they will adjust. People who care about the role you played will try to pull you back into it. That difference matters. Watch behavior, not words.

Anyone can say they want the best for you. Not everyone wants the version of you that comes with growth. Growth creates distance, independence, and unpredictability. That scares people who are used to having access to you.

Some people do not want you to be strong. They want you to be stable, familiar, accessible, available, and consistent in ways that serve them.

They will call that love. It is not.

It is comfort.

Love that requires you to stay the same is not love. It is control disguised as concern. It is attachment dressed up as loyalty.

This is why change reveals everything. When you start setting boundaries, choosing yourself, and moving differently, people show you exactly why they were in your life.

Some step forward, some step back, some get quiet, and some get loud. All of it is information.

The mistake is trying to convince people to love the new version of you. You do not need to sell your growth, justify your evolution, or explain why you cannot be who you used to be.

You already tried that version. It did not work. Let people grieve the old you. That is not your responsibility to manage. Grief is part of transition. You do not heal it by shrinking back. You are allowed to disappoint people who only felt comfortable when you were convenient, to change the terms of engagement, and to redefine who you are without taking a vote.

You are not betraying anyone by growing. You are honoring yourself.

And here is the part nobody tells you. Some people will never adjust. They will hold onto the old version of you forever, bring it up in conversations, remind you of who you used to be, and use nostalgia as a weapon.

That is their way of trying to resurrect a version of you that no longer exists.

Do not resurrect yourself to make others comfortable.

You are not here to preserve memories. You are here to build a future.

People love you based on the version of you that benefits them until you force them to confront who you are becoming. That confrontation separates real support from emotional dependency.

Let it separate.

Growth is not supposed to be universally accepted. It is supposed to be aligned.

The more honest you are about who you are becoming, the fewer people will have access to you. That is not a loss. That is refinement.

You do not need more people. You need the right ones.

And sometimes that means walking alone long enough to become the version of you that does not need to be validated.

Chapter 7

ACTION PLAN FOR CHANGE

1. Write down the roles you have played in your closest relationships: listener, fixer, provider, peacemaker, supporter. Roles form quietly. You're not assigned them—you grow into them.

2. Ask yourself which of those roles no longer align with who you are becoming. Misalignment doesn't mean the role was wrong. It means it has expired.

3. Choose one role to step back from immediately. Less fixing, less listening, less accommodating. Do not attempt a personality overhaul. Choose one role and reduce it by 20–30%.

4. Do not explain the change. Let behavior establish the new boundary. When you stop performing the role consistently, others are forced to adapt—or reveal dependency.

5. Observe who respects the shift and who resists it. Alignment reveals itself when benefits change.

You are not losing love. You are shedding dependency.

YOU ARE NOT REQUIRED TO CARRY OTHER PEOPLE'S COMFORT.

You are not required to carry other people's comfort

You have been walking around with emotional weight that was never yours to hold.

You carry other people's moods, their disappointments, their insecurities, their reactions, and their expectations. You adjust your tone to keep them calm, soften your truth to keep them comfortable, delay your decisions to avoid upsetting them, and rehearse conversations in your head just to make sure nobody feels uncomfortable.

That is not kindness. That is emotional labor you never signed up for.

You are not required to carry other people's comfort. Adults are responsible for regulating their own emotions.

Somewhere along the way, you took on a job that does not belong to you, and now you are exhausted, wondering why your life feels heavy.

Every time you censor yourself to protect someone else's feelings, you teach them that your truth is negotiable. Every time you shrink to avoid conflict, you reinforce the idea that their comfort matters more than your clarity. Over time, you disappear, and nobody even notices because you trained them to expect it.

You mistake peacekeeping for peace. They are not the same. Peacekeeping is fragile. It requires constant monitoring, constant adjusting, and constant silence. Peace is solid. It does not depend on everyone agreeing. It does not require you to perform emotional gymnastics to keep the room calm.

You cannot build peace while carrying other people's comfort.

The reason you feel tense around certain people is because you are on guard, anticipating their reactions, filtering your words, and managing their emotions before they even happen. That tension is your body telling you something is wrong.

You are not meant to be emotionally responsible for grown people.

People get uncomfortable when you change because your change forces them to deal with their own feelings instead of leaning on you to manage them. They feel exposed, uncertain, and left behind. Instead of sitting with those feelings, they project them onto you.

They say you are cold, selfish, or acting brand new. What they really mean is you stopped cushioning their discomfort.

You need to understand this. Discomfort is not harm. Someone feeling uncomfortable does not mean you did something wrong. Growth requires discomfort, boundaries create discomfort, and truth creates discomfort. That does not make them cruel. It makes them honest.

You have been conditioned to believe that if someone feels bad, it must be your fault. That belief makes you easy to control. All someone has to do is react emotionally, and you fold. That pattern ends here.

You are allowed to let people feel however they feel without rushing in to fix it, to say what needs to be said and let the reaction belong to them, and to choose yourself and allow others to process that choice on their own timeline.

You do not owe emotional cushioning.

The hardest part is trusting that relationships can survive honesty. The ones that cannot were not healthy to begin with. Real relationships adapt. Unhealthy ones rely on emotional management.

Watch what happens when you stop rescuing people from their feelings. Some will rise to the occasion. Others will accuse you of changing. That accusation is their way of trying to pull you back into emotional service.

Do not go back.

You have spent years prioritizing harmony over truth. Harmony without truth is a lie that eventually collapses. Truth might shake things initially, but it creates something real.

You are not here to maintain emotional comfort at the expense of your own life. You are here to live honestly. Comfort is optional. Truth is not.

Let people sit with their disappointment, process their reactions, feel confused, and adjust. Or not.

Their feelings are theirs.

Your responsibility is to live in alignment.

When you stop carrying other people's comfort, your life gets quieter. Not because people disappear but because the emotional noise fades. You stop anticipating reactions, walking on eggshells, and editing yourself.

That quiet is not loneliness. It is a relief.

You will notice who respects your honesty and who only respects your silence. That distinction matters more than you think.

You do not need to be harsh or cruel. You just need to stop cushioning reality. Say what you mean, do what aligns, and let the rest fall where it may.

Your job is not to keep everyone comfortable. Your job is to keep yourself honest.

Chapter 8

ACTION PLAN FOR CHANGE

1. Identify one relationship where you regularly manage the other person's emotions. Be specific. Name the person and the pattern.

2. Choose one truth you have been avoiding because of how they might react. If you've been rehearsing it silently, it's already overdue.

3. Say that truth calmly, without softening it to protect their comfort. State the truth once. Let it land.

4. Do not rush to explain or apologize for their reaction. Let them own it. Silence here is an act of trust—trust that they can feel what they feel without you managing it.

5. Notice how much lighter you feel when you stop carrying what is not yours. That feeling is your nervous system recalibrating to honesty.

Comfort is optional. Alignment is not.

EVERY EXPLANATION INVITES DEBATE.

Explaining yourself is a trap

Every time you explain yourself, you think you are creating clarity. What you are actually doing is asking for permission.

You explain because you want to be understood, because you want people to see your heart, and because you believe if you say it the right way, they will finally get it, and everything will smooth out. That belief has kept you stuck longer than you realize.

Explaining yourself is a trap.

It feels productive, but it keeps you stationary; it feels mature, but it weakens your position; and it feels like communication, but it is really negotiation with people who were never entitled to a vote in the first place.

Here is the truth you avoid: people who want to under-stand you do not need long explanations. People who do not want to understand you will never be convinced, no matter how carefully you speak.

So why are you still explaining? You explain because you are uncomfortable with being misunderstood. You explain because you want approval wrapped in agreement. You explain because silence makes you anxious, and disagree-ment makes you feel exposed. You explain because you are still emotionally attached to how others perceive you.

And that attachment costs you power.

Every explanation invites debate, every justification opens the door for opinions, and every clarification gives people space to push back, question, and reshape your deci-sion. Suddenly, what was your choice becomes a group dis-cussion, and you are back where you started.

Stuck.

You do not explain when you are certain. You explain when you are seeking reassurance. That is not a strength. That is doubt dressed up as communication.

Watch confident people closely. They do not overexplain. They state, move, and let actions speak. They understand that clarity comes from consistency, not conversation.

You keep trying to talk people into respecting your boundaries. Respect does not come from talking. It comes from enforcement.

You keep thinking that if you explain why you need space, people will honor it. They will not. They will hear reasons and look for loopholes, then push because explanations signal flexibility. Silence signals finality.

You are not required to convince anyone of your decisions. You are allowed to make choices and let them stand, to be misunderstood during transition, and to disappoint people without explaining yourself out of it.

Explanations feel safe because they keep you connected. But that connection is conditional. It requires you to keep talking, keep justifying, and keep managing reactions. That is not freedom. That is emotional labor.

Ask yourself this honestly: How many times have you explained the same decision to the same people, clarified your intentions only to be questioned again, or left conversations feeling drained, confused, or unsure, even though you were confident before you spoke?

That is the trap closing.

People who benefit from you staying accessible love explanations because explanations keep you engaged, keep you open, keep the door unlocked, and give them room to influence.

People who respect you do not need them.

You are not obligated to narrate your growth. You are not required to announce your boundaries. You are not responsible for making your choices digestible.

Let people sit with uncertainty, be confused, and form whatever story they want. You cannot control perception without losing yourself in the process.

The need to explain comes from fear of judgment. But judgment happens whether you explain or not. The only difference is how much energy you waste trying to manage it. Silence is uncomfortable because it removes your illusion of control. You think explaining gives you control over the outcome. It does not. It gives others access to your reasoning, which they then dissect, criticize, or dismiss.

Silence protects your direction.

This does not mean you never communicate. It means you stop overcommunicating, speak once clearly, and then move accordingly, and let repetition come from action, not conversation.

You do not need to announce every shift, defend every choice, or clarify every misunderstanding.

Your life is not a press conference.

The more you explain, the more you invite people into decisions that should have been private. The less you explain, the more authority you reclaim.

People will adjust, or they will fall away. Either outcome serves you.

The strongest position you can take is calm certainty without commentary. That kind of silence unsettles people who rely on your explanations to feel relevant.

Let them be unsettled.

You are not here to be interpreted. You are here to be aligned.

Explanations are a habit. Breaking them will feel uncomfortable at first. You will feel rude. You will feel cold. You will feel like you are doing something wrong. That feeling is withdrawal. You are detoxing from approval.

Give it time.

You will notice something shift. Conversations shorten, resistance fades, your mind clears, and your confidence stabilizes. People stop debating with you because there is nothing to debate.

That is when you know you are free.

Chapter 9

ACTION PLAN FOR CHANGE

1. Identify one area of your life where you consistently overexplain: relationships, work, family decisions, or boundaries. Notice where your sentences run long, where you stack reasons, where you feel the urge to pre-empt disagreement.

2. The next time the topic comes up, state your position once clearly and stop talking. Say it calmly. Then stop talking.

3. Do not justify, clarify, or add context. Let silence do the work. Let the other person sit with it.

4. If pressed, repeat the same sentence calmly or disengage completely. You are not required to perform endurance to prove sincerity.

5. Track how your energy changes over the next
    week when you stop explaining yourself. Notice
    the shift over a week. That data matters more
    than anyone's opinion.

Clarity comes from movement, not conversation.

YOU ARE NOT HERE TO BE MANAGEABLE. YOU ARE HERE TO MOVE.

They call it humble, because it keeps you manageable

Somewhere along the way, you were taught that wanting more was dangerous, that ambition should be quiet, that confidence should be muted, and that success should never make anyone else uncomfortable. They wrapped that lesson in a pretty word and called it humble.

What they really meant was manageable.

Humbleness has been weaponized against people who dare to want more than survival, against people who move with certainty, against people who speak clearly about their goals, and against people who refuse to shrink their vision to fit the room.

You were told to tone it down, to stay grounded, to be realistic, to not get ahead of yourself, and to remember where you came from. And you listened because it sounded responsible, mature, and wise.

But look closely. Every time someone told you to be humble, it was right when you were about to expand, stepping into something unfamiliar, when your confidence started to show, or when your ambition became visible.

That is not a coincidence.

False humility is control disguised as character. It is used to keep you digestible, predictable, and from outgrowing the environment you are in. People do not fear arrogance. They fear displacement, the feeling that you no longer need their approval, and losing relevance in your life.

Real humility has nothing to do with shrinking. Real humility is knowing who you are without needing to announce it or deny it. It does not require you to dim your light, ask you to minimize your goals, or force you to apologize for wanting more.

False humility tells you to make yourself smaller, so others feel comfortable standing next to you.

You have mistaken insecurity management for morality.

Watch how often humility is demanded only when someone starts to rise. Nobody asks you to be humble when you are struggling, lost, or invisible. Humility only becomes a requirement when you are gaining traction.

That should tell you everything.

You do not owe anyone smallness. You do not owe anyone comfort at the expense of your growth. You do not owe anyone access to a version of you that no longer exists.

Confidence does not make you arrogant, clarity does not make you disrespectful, and wanting more does not make you ungrateful. Those labels are assigned by people who are uncomfortable with change.

You keep second-guessing yourself because you internalized these messages. You lower your voice when you talk about your goals. You add jokes to soften your ambition. You downplay wins so nobody feels threatened. You sabotage momentum by pretending you are not serious.

Then you wonder why people do not take you seriously.

You trained them not to.

There is a difference between arrogance and ownership. Arrogance needs validation while ownership needs alignment. Arrogance compares while ownership commits. Arrogance performs while ownership moves.

You are allowed to own your direction without apology.

False humility keeps you manageable, not just to others but to yourself. You start editing your own thoughts, negotiating your own dreams, questioning your instincts, and confusing fear with wisdom.

That internal management is more damaging than external criticism.

You do not need to announce your ambition to everyone. But you also do not need to hide it from yourself, need permission to want a bigger life, or need approval to pursue it.

People will say you changed when you stop shrinking. They will say success got to your head, that you forgot who you are, or that money, power, growth, and attention ruined you.

What they are really saying is you no longer fit where they placed you.

Let them talk.

Your job is not to be manageable. Your job is to be effective.

The people who respect you will not ask you to shrink. They will challenge you to sharpen, push you to refine, not retreat, and celebrate your growth even when it highlights their own need to evolve.

The ones who demand humility as silence and ambition as arrogance are revealing their ceiling.

You do not need to adopt it.

You were not meant to live a life that requires constant reassurance to others. You were meant to build something that speaks for itself.

Stop apologizing for wanting more, minimizing what matters to you, and confusing comfort with virtue.

Manageability is not a goal.

Alignment is.

Chapter 10

ACTION PLAN FOR CHANGE

1. Identify one area where you consistently downplay your ambition or confidence to make others comfortable. Be precise. Downplaying is almost always strategic, not accidental.

2. Write down what you actually want in that area without softening the language. If it makes you slightly uncomfortable to read, you're doing it right.

3. Stop joking about it. Stop minimizing it. Speak about it plainly at least once this week. You don't need to convince. You only need to state.

4. Notice who reacts with support and who reacts with discomfort. That reaction reveals alignment.

Discomfort may show up as jokes, deflection, advice you didn't ask for, or subtle dismissal.

5. Commit to honoring your ambition privately and publicly without apology for the next thirty days. Let your ambition take up its natural space.

You are not here to be manageable. You are here to move.

YOU ARE NOT COLD. YOU ARE CLEAR. CLARITY SHUTS ALL OF THAT DOWN.

FXCK THEM does not mean you are cold, it means you are clear

People keep confusing clarity with cruelty because clarity removes access.

When you stop explaining, stop bending, and stop adjusting your tone to manage reactions.

People do not say you became focused. They say you became cold.

That label is not an accident. It is a defense mechanism.

Cold is what people call you when they can no longer reach you the way they used to, what they say when emotional manipulation stops working, and the word they use when your boundaries finally hold.

You are not cold. You are clear.

Clarity feels harsh to people who benefited from your confusion. When you were unsure they could influence you, when you hesitated they could redirect you, when you over-explained they could negotiate, and when you cared too much they could pull on guilt.

Clarity shuts all of that down.

And people hate losing leverage.

So they say you changed, that you are distant, heartless, acting brand-new, or that you do not care anymore.

What they really mean is you stopped letting them blur your direction.

You spent years being emotionally flexible. You bent so much that people started expecting it. They got used to you making space for their feelings, even when it cost you peace. They got used to you adjusting your life so theirs stayed comfortable. They got used to you absorbing pressure, so they never had to feel it.

Clarity sounds like no without an explanation, silence instead of justification, and consistency instead of conversation.

And that makes people uncomfortable because it removes their ability to argue.

Cold people withdraw. Clear people decide.

There is a difference, and you need to internalize it.

Being cold is shutting down emotionally because you are hurt, resentful, or afraid. Being clear is staying open while refusing to be controlled. Being cold is reactive, while being clear is intentional.

You are not withdrawing because you are wounded. You are withdrawing because you are focused.

That distinction matters.

When you stop reacting emotionally to opinions, people lose their power over you; when you stop explaining yourself, people stop debating with you; and when you stop trying to be understood, people either adjust or disappear.

That is not cruelty. That is filtration.

The reason clarity feels aggressive to others is that it does not ask permission, negotiate, or soften itself to be accepted. It simply exists.

And people who rely on access interpret that as rejection.

You have to be strong enough to let people misunderstand you while you stay aligned, disciplined enough to let narratives form without trying to correct them, and grounded enough to let silence speak.

This is where most people fold. They hear cold and panic. They rush to explain that they still care, that they are not mad, that they are just busy, that nothing is wrong, and that they still love them.

And the moment they do that, clarity collapses.

You do not need to prove warmth to people who only respected your availability.

Your life is not meant to be constantly emotionally or physically accessible. You are allowed to have seasons where you are unavailable, to prioritize yourself without announcing it, and to move quietly without reassurance.

Clarity does not mean you stop caring. It means you stop over-caring, care with structure, care with limits, and care without sacrificing yourself.

People who are emotionally healthy will recognize clarity and respect it. People who are dependent on your flexibility will fight it.

That fight is not your responsibility.

You cannot be clear and liked by everyone. The desire to be liked will always compete with the need to be clear. One has to lose.

You already know which one you have been choosing.

That choice kept you stuck.

Clarity is what allows you to move without dragging guilt behind you, to say no without rehearsing, to protect your time without apology, and to show up fully where it matters instead of partially everywhere.

The calm you feel when you stop explaining is not coldness but relief. The distance you feel when you stop reacting is not emptiness but space. The quiet you experience when you stop managing emotions is not loneliness but peace.

People who truly value you will feel the shift and adjust. People who valued access will call you cold.

Let them.

Cold is just the word people use when they are no longer centered in your life.

You do not owe warmth to people who confuse access with love, softness to people who only respect you when you bend, or emotional availability to anyone who drains you.

Clarity is not cruelty. It is maturity. And maturity always offends people who benefited from your immaturity. Stand firm. Do not flinch when the labels come, correct the narrative, or rush to soften.

Let your consistency teach what your words never could.

Chapter 11

ACTION PLAN FOR CHANGE

1. Identify one area of your life where people have labeled you cold for setting boundaries or changing behavior. Being called "cold" is often feedback from someone experiencing reduced access, not reduced care.

2. Ask yourself honestly whether you became cruel or simply became clear. If you didn't attack, belittle, or retaliate—you weren't cruel. You were clear.

3. Stop defending your clarity. No explanations. No reassurance tours. Let the behavior stand on its own.

4. Practice responding less emotionally and more intentionally for the next two weeks. Your nervous system will resist at first. Stay steady.

5. Notice who adapts and who resists. Respect follows clarity. Control resists it.

You are not cold. You are finally clear.

PEOPLE WILL SURVIVE BEING DISAPPOINTED.

YOU WILL NOT SURVIVE BETRAYING YOURSELF FOREVER.

The real fear is not failure, it is disappointing people who expect you to stay the same

You tell yourself you are afraid to fail. That sounds responsible, honest, and like self-awareness. It is also not true.

If failure was really your fear, you would not be stuck. You would be experimenting, trying, risking, and moving, even if the outcome was uncertain.

The real fear is disappointing people who expect you to stay the same.

Failure is private while disappointment is public. Failure happens in your own head while disappointment shows up in faces, voices, texts, silence, and judgment. Failure hurts your pride while disappointment threatens your identity.

You are not afraid of falling short. You are afraid of changing the relationship dynamics that keep you accepted.

You are afraid of what happens when people realize you are no longer who they thought you were, afraid of the conversations that follow, the looks, the questions, the shift in tone, the subtle distance, the awkwardness, and the disappointment.

That fear keeps you manageable.

People have expectations of you based on who you have been: the dependable one, the consistent one, the available one, the predictable one, the version that fits into their life without disruption. When you change, you break an unspoken contract.

And broken contracts make people uncomfortable.

You feel that discomfort before it even happens. You imagine it, rehearse it, and try to avoid it by staying the same. You tell yourself it is loyalty, patience, or timing.

It is fear.

You are afraid that if you choose differently, people will feel let down, take it personally, question your character, withdraw support or affection, or see you as selfish, ungrateful, or cold.

So you stay.

You stay in jobs you have outgrown, in relationships that no longer align, and in routines that drain you.

You stay small because acceptance feels safer than honesty.

Failure would only disappoint you. Change disappoints others. And right now, you care more about them than you do about your future.

That is the truth most people never say out loud.

You are not responsible for meeting expectations that were built around an outdated version of you, not obligated to stay the same to preserve someone else's comfort, and not required to live a life that makes sense to people who are not living it.

Disappointment is part of growth.

As you evolve, people have to update their view of you. Some will and some will not. The ones who cannot will try to pull you back by reminding you of who you used to be. They will say you are different, as if it were an insult, or that you changed, as if it were a flaw.

You did.

That is the point.

You have been so focused on not letting others down that you have repeatedly let yourself down. You delayed your life so nobody else had to adjust, carried expectations that were never yours to fulfill, and made choices based on who people needed you to be instead of who you are becoming.

And now you feel stuck, resentful, and restless.

That feeling is not confusion. It is misalignment.

The discomfort you are avoiding by staying the same will be replaced by a deeper regret if you do not move. One day, you will look back and realize you lived someone else's expectations instead of your own potential. That regret will hurt more than any disappointment you caused by choosing yourself.

People will survive being disappointed. You will not survive betraying yourself forever.

Let them be surprised, confused, and disappointed.

Those reactions are temporary. The damage of staying small is permanent.

You do not owe consistency to people who are not evolving with you. You owe honesty to yourself. Growth requires you to break expectations, and if you meet every expectation placed on you, you will never become anything new.

Expectations are comfortable cages.

You have to decide which pain you are willing to live with. The pain of disappointing others now or the pain of disappointing yourself later.

One leads to freedom. The other leads to resentment.

The people who truly care about you will adjust. They might struggle, but they will respect your truth, while the ones who only cared about the role you played will resist and guilt you.

That resistance is confirmation.

You are not selfish for choosing a life that fits you. You are responsible.

Failure is not what you fear. You have failed before and survived, but you have not fully stepped into who you are becoming, regardless of who it disappoints.

That is the real work.

And that work starts when you stop letting other people's expectations dictate your choices.

Chapter 12

ACTION PLAN FOR CHANGE

1. Write down one expectation others have of you that no longer aligns with who you are becoming. Write it plainly. Naming it turns it from an invisible pressure into a conscious constraint.

2. Identify the decision you have been avoiding because it might disappoint someone. Avoided decisions don't disappear—they just charge interest.

3. Ask yourself which disappointment you can live with longer: theirs or yours. One of these disappointments compounds. The other fades.

4. Take one step this week toward that decision without announcing it or seeking reassurance.

Behavior changes reality faster than declarations ever do.

5. Sit with the discomfort instead of running from it. Discomfort is temporary. Regret lasts. Discomfort is the nervous system adjusting to honesty.

Disappointing others is sometimes the price of becoming yourself.

DISTANCE DOES NOT RUIN RELATIONSHIPS.

IT EXPOSES THEM.

Chapter 13

Distance reveals everything

You do not really know people when they have unlimited access to you. You know them when that access changes.

Distance does not ruin relationships. It exposes them.

When you step back, stop initiating, stop checking in, stop explaining, and stop showing up out of habit instead of intention, that is when the truth surfaces. Not through words but through behavior.

Distance removes performance.

As long as you are present, people can pretend. They can say the right things, maintain the image, and benefit from your energy without acknowledging it. Distance takes all of that away. What remains is real.

You have been afraid of distance because you were taught it equals abandonment, that stepping back is unkind, that creating space is cold, and that pulling away means you do not care. That belief kept you overextending long after relationships stopped being mutual.

Distance is not punishment. It is a test. When you stop showing up, who notices? When you stop calling, who reaches out? When you stop explaining, who is left to respect your choice?

Those answers matter more than any conversation you could have.

You cannot see the imbalance while you are standing inside it. You have to step away to notice who was leaning on you and who was walking with you. Distance creates a perspective that closeness never will.

People who value you will adjust. They might ask questions, feel the shift, or need time. But they will respect your space and meet you where you are. People who valued your access will panic, guilt you, accuse you of changing, and distance themselves from you.

That reaction is information.

You do not need to confront it, correct it, or do anything but observe it.

Distance also reveals something else. How much of your exhaustion came from maintaining connections that no longer served you? When you step back, and your body feels lighter, that is not a coincidence. That is your nervous system finally relaxing.

You have been carrying conversations, obligations, expectations, and emotional labor that should have been shared. Distance removes your contribution, revealing what remains.

Sometimes nothing remains.

That realization hurts because it forces you to accept that some relationships were held together by your effort alone. But that pain is honest. And honest pain is better than a comfortable illusion.

You have to stop measuring relationships by history and start measuring them by reciprocity. Distance shows you who fills the space and who waits for you to return to fill it again.

You are not obligated to return.

The fear you feel when you create distance is not loneliness. It is identity withdrawal. You are used to being needed. You are used to being involved. You are used to being the connector. When you step back, you do not know who you are without that role.

That is why distance feels uncomfortable at first.

But that discomfort is where growth lives.

Distance gives you time to hear yourself again. To feel your own rhythm. To remember what you like, what you want, what you need, when nobody else is pulling on you. It reconnects you to your own life.

You cannot build clarity while constantly being influenced. Distance reduces influence.

People who respect you will not punish you for taking space, demand access, rush you, or weaponize your absence. They will understand that space is sometimes necessary for growth.

The ones who do not will reveal themselves quickly.

Distance is not something you explain. It is something you allow. You do not announce it or justify it. You simply step back and let reality speak for itself.

What you learn in that space will change how you move forever.

You will see who reaches for you and who only reaches through you, who values you and who values what you provide, and who respects your boundaries and who resents them.

Distance reveals everything because it removes distraction.

If a relationship cannot survive distance, it was never stable to begin with. Stability does not require constant contact. It requires mutual respect.

You are not required to stay close to prove love. You are allowed to step back to protect clarity.

Distance is not abandonment. It is honesty without conversation.

And once you see the truth, you cannot unsee it.

Chapter 13

ACTION PLAN FOR CHANGE

1. Choose one relationship where you feel drained, confused, or obligated rather than supported. Name the relationship honestly. Confusion is often the first signal of misalignment.

2. Create intentional distance for two weeks through less initiating, less responding, and less explaining. You're not disappearing—you're removing effort and observing what remains.

3. Observe without reacting. Notice who respects the space and who resents it. This is the hardest part. Just watch.

4. Pay attention to how your body feels during the distance; lighter or heavier tells you everything. Lighter means alignment. Heavier means cost.

5. Decide what level of access makes sense moving forward based on behavior, not history. Let the decision come from evidence, not obligation.

Distance is not about pushing people away. It is about seeing clearly who belongs.

RESPECT IS FELT WHEN SOMEONE HEARS NO AND STOPS.

Chapter 14

Respect is felt before it is spoken

You have been waiting for the announcement of respect. That is why you keep missing it.

Respect does not come through words, arrive as compliments, or show up as reassurance. Respect is felt and experienced. It shows up in behavior long before it appears in language.

People who respect you do not test your boundaries, push after you say no, ask for explanations, or need reminders. They adjust.

You have confused politeness with respect. Someone can speak kindly and still disregard your time, praise you and still violate your boundaries, or say they love you and still ignore what matters to you.

Respect is not what people say when you are present. It is how they move when you are not.

You feel disrespected because you are constantly being interrupted, questioned, second-guessed, and negotiated with. You feel unheard because people listen to respond, not to understand. You feel overlooked because your needs are treated as optional while everyone else's are treated as urgent.

That is not a misunderstanding. That is information.

People treat you based on what they believe you will tolerate. Not based on what you deserve.

Read that again.

Respect is not demanded. It is enforced. And enforcement does not require aggression. It requires consistency.

You have been trying to earn respect by being reasonable, flexible, patient, and understanding. You thought that if you explained clearly enough, compromised often enough, and stayed calm long enough, people would finally value you.

That is not how respect works.

Respect comes when people realize you will not move for convenience, that your boundaries are not suggestions, that your no does not soften under pressure, and that your silence does not mean weakness.

The reason some people keep pushing you is because they have learned you eventually give in. You eventually explain. You eventually adjust. You eventually accommodate.

So they wait.

And every time you fold, you teach them exactly how far they can go.

Respect is felt the moment someone realizes you are serious about your time, your boundaries, and your direction.

You do not need to announce seriousness. You demonstrate it through behavior.

When you stop responding immediately, stop negotiating, and stop repeating yourself, people notice.

They may not like it. But they feel it.

That feeling is respect.

You keep seeking verbal confirmation because you do not yet trust yourself. You want someone else to validate that you are allowed to stand firm. You want reassurance that you are not being unreasonable.

You do not need permission to be respected.

People who truly respect you will not need explanations. They will not guilt you. They will not test you. They will not pressure you. They will not make you feel bad for protecting yourself.

People who do not respect you will disguise pressure as concern and persistence as care.

Learn to tell the difference.

Respect is quiet. It does not argue, debate, or push. It adapts.

Disrespect is loud. It questions, challenges, negotiates, and demands access.

If you have to constantly explain your boundaries, they are not being respected. If you have to remind people of your limits, they are not listening, and if you feel drained after interactions, that is your answer.

Stop waiting for respect to be spoken. Start paying attention to how people behave when your boundaries are in place.

Respect is felt when someone hears no and stops, when someone adjusts without resentment, and when someone honors your time without complaint.

You do not have to convince people to respect you. You have to decide that you will not continue engaging with behavior that does not.

That decision will change how people treat you faster than any conversation ever could.

Once you feel real respect, you will never settle for performative kindness again. You will stop confusing friendliness with honor. You will stop mistaking words for alignment.

You will start trusting how your body reacts instead of how people explain themselves.

Your body knows when it is respected and relaxes. Your body knows when it is not and tightens.

Pay attention.

Respect does not need to be loud to be real. And when it is missing, no amount of talking will create it.

You do not chase respect. You live in a way that makes disrespect impossible to ignore.

Chapter 14

ACTION PLAN FOR CHANGE

1. Identify one relationship or environment where you feel consistently drained or dismissed. Be specific: the person, the environment, the recurring pattern.

2. Observe behavior, not words, for one week. No confronting. No explaining. Words are easy. Behavior is costly. This week gathers data.

3. Set one clear boundary and enforce it without discussion. Boundaries are not requests. They're conditions.

4. Watch how the other person responds. Adjustment is respect. Resistance is information. You don't need to label it. You don't need to explain it. Just note it.

5. Decide what level of access is appropriate based on how your boundary is handled. Let behavior—not sentiment—set the terms.

Respect is not something you ask for. It is something you either allow or deny through your actions.

YOU DID NOT DISAPPEAR. YOU ARRIVED.

You are allowed to choose yourself repeatedly even when people get tired of it

You thought choosing yourself was a one-time decision. That once you did it, everyone would adjust, understand, and move on. That belief is why you keep folding.

Choosing yourself is not a moment. It is a practice. And people get tired of it quickly.

They were fine with it the first time because they assumed it was temporary. They thought you just needed space. They thought it was a phase. They thought you would come back to normal. When they realize this is who you are, now the pressure starts.

That is when choosing yourself gets uncomfortable.

People do not get upset because you chose yourself once. They get upset when you keep choosing yourself. When it becomes consistent. When it stops being negotiable. When they realize the old access is gone for good.

Consistency exposes entitlement.

You will feel the shift when people start testing you. They ask again after you said no, bring it up casually, joke about your boundaries, pretend not to remember, and frame your choices as temporary inconveniences instead of permanent changes.

That is not confusion. That is resistance.

You are allowed to choose yourself again, even when they sigh, roll their eyes, act disappointed, imply you are being difficult, or remind you of how you used to be.

Especially then.

Choosing yourself once can be written off. Repeatedly choosing yourself forces people to adjust or exit. That is why it feels heavier, why guilt shows up stronger, and why you question yourself more the second, third, and fourth time.

You are not wrong. You are just no longer flexible.

People benefited from your inconsistency. They waited you out, knowing that if they applied enough pressure, you would eventually cave. When you stop caving, they have to face the new reality.

And that reality does not center them.

You need to understand this. People get tired of your growth not because it harms them but because it limits their influence. Every time you choose yourself, you remove a lever they used to pull. Over time, they feel the loss of control and react emotionally.

Do not mistake emotional reaction for moral feedback.

You do not need to rotate back to make others comfortable, alternate between growth and guilt, or balance choosing yourself with self-betrayal to prove you are still kind.

Kindness that costs you yourself is not kindness. It is fear.

You keep asking how long you can choose yourself before it becomes selfish. The answer is simple. As long as it takes.

People who respect you will adjust. They may not love every change, but they will accept it, while people who relied on your self-sacrifice will get tired of waiting for you to revert.

Let them get tired.

You do not owe anyone access to the old you, consistency to versions of relationships that no longer fit, or explanations for continuing to honor boundaries you already communicated.

Repetition is not cruelty. It is clarity.

The strongest form of self-respect is choosing yourself again after the novelty wears off, after the applause fades, after the encouragement stops, after the guilt starts, and after the comments come.

That is when growth becomes real.

You will notice something powerful when you keep choosing yourself. The anxiety decreases, the need to explain fades, and the urge to justify disappears. You stop rehearsing conversations, bracing for reactions, and living on edge.

Your nervous system learns it is safe to stay aligned.

Choosing yourself repeatedly builds trust in yourself. And that trust is what most people lack. They doubt themselves because they have a history of abandoning their own needs the moment pressure appears.

Break that pattern.

Every time you choose yourself again, you rewrite that history.

People will say you are stubborn, inflexible, set in your ways, or that you changed.

You did. You stopped negotiating with your own life.

You are not required to be endlessly accommodating, to prove your growth by suffering through guilt, or to explain why the same boundary still exists.

The same boundary exists because you do.

Choosing yourself repeatedly is how you build a life that feels stable instead of reactive, how you stop oscillating between confidence and doubt, and how you stop being pulled in multiple directions.

It is how you finally become solid.

And solidity makes people uncomfortable because it cannot be manipulated.

That discomfort is not your problem.

Your job is not to manage how others feel about your growth. Your job is to live it consistently.

Choose yourself today.

Choose yourself tomorrow.

Choose yourself again when they test you.

That repetition is the work.

Chapter 15

ACTION PLAN FOR CHANGE

1. Identify one boundary you have already set but struggled to maintain consistently. This is the boundary you set, meant, and then slowly eroded.

2. Write down the moments when you felt pressured to bend and why you did. You didn't fail—you responded to discomfort. Now you're choosing differently.

3. Decide now that the next time it is tested, you will hold it without explanation. Holding the boundary calmly teaches others how serious it is—and teaches you that you can trust yourself.

4. Practice choosing yourself daily in one small way for the next week through time, space, rest, or

focus. You are training your nervous system to associate self-respect with safety.

5. Notice how your confidence grows each time you choose yourself again. Each time you choose yourself and nothing collapses, your trust in yourself strengthens.

You do not have to choose yourself once. You have to choose yourself until it feels normal. Every boundary you hold becomes evidence that you are reliable—to yourself.

YOUR WORTH IS NOT MEASURED BY ACCESS. IT IS MEASURED BY ALIGNMENT.

Being liked is not a life goal

At some point, you confused popularity with progress. That confusion cost you years.

You were taught early that being liked meant you were doing something right, that approval was safety, and that acceptance was success. So you learned how to read rooms, how to adjust your tone, how to say the right thing, how to be agreeable, and how to avoid rocking the boat.

You became likable.

And stuck.

Being liked is not a life goal. It is a social side effect that people mistake for achievement. Likes do not build futures. Approval does not create direction. Popularity does not equal purpose.

You can be liked and miserable, liked and stagnant, or liked and invisible to yourself.

Most people who chase being liked never build anything meaningful because building requires friction. And friction threatens approval.

The need to be liked keeps you safe but small, agreeable instead of decisive, available instead of focused, and responsive instead of intentional.

You keep asking yourself why you feel unfulfilled, even though people seem to like you. That is because liking does not satisfy the part of you that wants to grow. It only feeds the part of you that wants to belong.

Belonging without alignment is a cage.

When being liked becomes a priority, you start editing your life in real time. You make choices based on reactions instead of values, measure success by applause instead of progress, and abandon instincts the moment they might offend someone.

That is not living. That is performing.

People who are liked by everyone usually stand for nothing specific. They are flexible enough to fit anywhere and grounded nowhere. That flexibility looks kind on the outside but feels hollow on the inside.

You do not need to be liked. You need to respect yourself.

The people you admire most were not universally liked while they were building. They were questioned, criticized, misunderstood, and doubted. Approval came later or not at all. But direction came first.

You have to decide which one you want.

Being liked requires you to stay readable, predictable, and non-threatening. Building a life that matters requires you to be decisive, unapologetic, and sometimes misunderstood.

Those two goals do not coexist.

The desire to be liked sneaks into everything: your career, your relationships, your boundaries, your opinions, and your silence. You hesitate not because you do not know what to do, but because you are calculating reactions.

That calculation is exhausting.

You were not meant to crowdsource your life. You were meant to direct it.

Being liked is temporary. It shifts with moods, trends, and convenience. The same people who like you today will criticize you tomorrow if it suits them. Basing your life on that is unstable.

Self-respect is stable.

When you stop trying to be liked, you gain something better: authority, calm, and focus. You stop explaining yourself, chasing validation, and feeling whiplash from other people's opinions.

You become solid.

Solid people do not need to be liked. They need to be aligned.

Some people will stop liking you when you stop accommodating them. That is not a loss. That is clarity. It shows you who was attached to your flexibility instead of your character.

You will notice that as you let go of being liked, your circle gets smaller but stronger, conversations get shorter but deeper, and energy gets quieter but steadier.

That trade is worth it.

You are not here to be agreeable. You are here to be effective.

Effectiveness requires decisions that not everyone will applaud, boundaries that not everyone will respect, and movement that not everyone will understand.

If you need everyone to like you, you will never move far enough to matter.

Let people misunderstand you, mislabel you, and be disappointed.

None of that determines your worth. Being liked is fragile. Alignment is durable. You do not need permission to stop auditioning for approval. You can walk off that stage right now.

The moment you stop trying to be liked, you start living for real.

Chapter 16

ACTION PLAN FOR CHANGE

---

1. Identify one area where you consistently prioritize being liked over being honest. Be specific. Liking is seductive because it feels like safety—but it often comes at the expense of self-respect.

2. Write down the truth you have been avoiding because of how it might be received. If it feels slightly sharp on the page, it's honest.

3. Act on that truth this week without seeking validation or reassurance. Do not poll others. Do not look for reassurance.

4. Notice who respects your decision, even if they do not like it. Some people won't like the

decision—but still respect it. That distinction matters.

5. Remind yourself daily that approval is not progress and alignment is the goal. You're not here to be liked by everyone. You're here to live inside your own decisions without resentment.

Being liked will never fulfill you. Living in alignment will.

YOU STOP
EXPLAINING
AND START
EXECUTING.

The day you stop seeking permission

There is a moment most people never reach, not because it is hidden or complicated, but because it requires a level of honesty most people avoid.

That moment is when you stop seeking permission.

Not verbally. You already know better than to ask out-right. You seek permission in subtler ways by hinting, testing reactions, floating ideas, waiting for encouragement, looking for signs, reading the room, and asking questions you already know the answers to.

You call it being thoughtful. It is not. It is hesitation disguised as consideration.

Seeking permission is how people delay their lives without admitting it.

You learned early that approval equals safety, that agreement equals acceptance, and that moving with consensus keeps you protected from judgment, rejection, and isolation. So you trained yourself to look outward before moving inward. You learned to wait until it felt safe enough to act.

That training never expires unless you actively unlearn it.

You keep thinking there will be a moment when it feels right, when everyone understands, when the timing is perfect, and when the reactions are supportive. That moment does not exist.

Permission is not something you receive. It is something you stop needing.

The day you stop seeking permission is the day your life speeds up. Not because obstacles disappear but because hesitation does. You stop pausing for reactions, checking temperature, and asking how this will land. You start asking where this leads.

That shift is quiet but violent.

It breaks the habit of deferring your life to other people's comfort, ends the loop of waiting for validation, and exposes how much time you wasted standing still with good intentions.

You will feel fear when you stop seeking permission. That fear is not danger. It is withdrawal. You are detoxing from external validation. Your nervous system has been trained to feel unsafe without consensus. That discomfort passes if you do not run from it.

Most people run back to permission because it feels familiar. They retreat to conversations that keep them tethered, ask one more opinion, seek one more sign, and tell themselves they are being smart.

They are scared.

When you stop seeking permission, people notice immediately. Not because you announce it, but because your energy changes. You move without checking, decide without explaining, and act without rehearsing.

That unsettles people.

Some will accuse you of being impulsive, others will say you are reckless, some will say you are rushing, and some will say you are not thinking things through. Those comments are not about your behavior. They are about their discomfort with your independence.

People are comfortable when you wait. They are uncomfortable when you move.

The irony is that the same people who caution you now will claim they always believed in you later if you succeed. That is how permission seekers are rewarded. With hindsight, praise and delayed validation.

You do not need either.

You are not irresponsible for trusting yourself. You are not arrogant for deciding without consensus. You are not wrong for moving before others are ready.

You have been ready longer than you admit.

The permission you are waiting for will never come because it is not external. It is internal. It comes the moment you accept that no one is coming to authorize your life, no one is going to tap you on the shoulder and say, "Now is the time," and no one is responsible for green-lighting your future.

That responsibility is yours.

Once you stop seeking permission, you realize how much of your anxiety came from anticipation, not action. The fear lived in the waiting. The tension lived in the delay. Movement dissolves both.

You will still make mistakes. That does not change. But mistakes made in motion teach faster than mistakes avoided through paralysis. Growth requires action, not consensus.

The day you stop seeking permission, you reclaim authority over your time, energy, and direction. You stop asking life for approval and start giving yourself instructions.

That is adulthood.

You do not need agreement to act, validation to decide, or reassurance to move.

You need honesty and courage.

Everything else is noise.

The longer you wait, the harder it becomes to start, the more opinions you collect, the weaker your instinct becomes, and the more permission you seek, the less you trust yourself.

Break that cycle now.

Do not announce it. Do not explain it. Do not justify it.

Just move.

Chapter 17

ACTION PLAN FOR CHANGE

1. Identify one decision you have been delaying while waiting for approval, reassurance, or signs. If you're honest, the delay isn't confusion. It's hesitation about owning the outcome. Name the decision exactly as it is.

2. Write down what you already know is the right move without asking anyone. Write it down plainly. This is not a brainstorm—it's a recognition.

3. Take one concrete step toward that decision within forty-eight hours. Action closes the loop that overthinking keeps open.

4. Do not discuss it with anyone until after the action is taken. Once the step is taken, you

can choose what to share—from stability, not uncertainty.

5. Notice how your confidence grows when action replaces permission. Confidence doesn't come from certainty. It comes from movement without permission.

The moment you stop asking is the moment your life starts moving again. Signs don't create clarity. Action does.

YOU STOP REACTING AND START RESPONDING.

Chapter 18

Let them misunderstand you

You have wasted an unbelievable amount of energy trying to be understood by people who were never meant to understand you.

You explain yourself, hoping clarity will soften judgment, repeat yourself, hoping tone will fix perception, and adjust language, hoping intention will land clean. And when it still does not, you feel frustrated, confused, and exposed.

Here is the truth you keep avoiding. Some people are not confused. They are committed to misunderstanding you.

Misunderstanding gives them comfort. It allows them to keep their narrative. It protects their ego. It excuses their inaction. If they truly understood you, they would have to confront themselves.

So they do not.

They simplify you, label you, and reduce your decisions to arrogance, impatience, selfishness, or ego. They ignore context, skip nuance, and flatten your growth into something they can dismiss.

And you keep trying to correct them.

That is the trap.

Not everyone deserves clarity. Some people only want confirmation of what they already believe. When you try to be understood by them, you are negotiating with someone who is not listening.

You need to understand this deeply. Being misunderstood is not a flaw. It is a consequence of growth.

When you change faster than people update their perception, you become unfamiliar; when you stop performing, you become unreadable; and when you stop explaining, you remove context. That absence of context makes people uncomfortable.

So they fill it in themselves.

You cannot control that process. And trying to will cost you your peace.

You were never meant to be universally understood. You were meant to be aligned. Understanding comes from proximity, experience, and shared values. If those are missing, misunderstanding is inevitable.

The problem is not that they misunderstand you. The problem is that you care too much about what they do.

You think misunderstanding threatens your reputation. It does not. Inconsistency, panic, over-explanation, and living out of alignment do.

Strong people are misunderstood all the time. Not because they are unclear but because they are uncompromising. Their clarity threatens the sense of safety of people who rely on flexibility.

Misunderstanding is often the price of independence.

You keep wanting people to see your heart. To recognize your intentions. To know you are not malicious. That desire keeps you emotionally tethered to people who are not walking your path.

They were never the assignment.

The assignment is your life, your growth, and your direction.

Anyone who does not align with that does not require clarification. They require distance.

You do not owe everyone access to your inner world, explanations for your choices, or comfort with your evolution.

Let people misunderstand you and keep moving.

That sentence scares you because you believe misunderstanding leads to isolation. It does not. It leads to filtration. The people who are meant to walk with you will ask questions respectfully. They will observe before judging. They will seek understanding without demanding it.

The rest will assume.

Let them.

You are not obligated to interrupt their assumptions, not responsible for correcting every false narrative, and not required to manage how people interpret your growth.

Silence is not weakness here. It is discipline.

The more you try to be understood, the more you reveal insecurity. The more you allow misunderstanding, the more authority you gain. Authority does not argue. It moves.

This is one of the hardest lessons because it requires you to let go of control over your perception. You cannot curate your image and live freely at the same time. One has to go.

Choose freedom.

People will say things about you that are not true. They will mislabel your boundaries, misunderstand your silence, question your motives, and create stories.

Those stories only matter if you stop moving to address them.

The fastest way to correct a misunderstanding is not a conversation. It is consistency. Live aligned long enough, and the truth becomes obvious without explanation.

And even if it does not, you will still be free.

You are not here to be interpreted. You are here to build.

Misunderstanding feels uncomfortable because it triggers the old part of you that needed approval to feel safe. That part is no longer in charge.

You are.

Let them misunderstand you.

Let them talk.

Let them assume.

Chapter 18

ACTION PLAN FOR CHANGE

---

1. Identify one situation where you are over-explaining because you want to be understood. Be specific about the person or context. Patterns live in particulars.

2. Stop explaining immediately. Let your actions speak instead. This is the hardest shift—and the most revealing.

3. When the urge to correct perception arises, pause and ask yourself who benefits from this explanation. That urge is reflexive. Pause before obeying it.

4. Commit to consistency over conversation for the next thirty days. Consistency does what conversation cannot: it removes ambiguity.

5. Notice how much lighter your mind feels when you stop managing narratives. That lightness is not avoidance—it's relief from unnecessary labor.

Understanding is optional. Alignment is mandatory. People who want to understand you will watch. People who want control will demand explanations.

AUTHORITY IS RETURNING TO WHERE IT ALWAYS BELONGED — YOU.

Chapter 19

Your life will get quieter, and that is the point

When you stop explaining yourself, stop reacting to every opinion, stop carrying other people's comfort, and stop seeking permission, your life gets quiet.

That quiet scares people who are used to chaos. It may scare you, too, at first.

You were conditioned to believe noise equals connection, that constant conversation means things are alive, and that silence means something is wrong. So when your phone stops buzzing, your calendar clears, and your mind finally slows down, you feel uneasy.

You think you lost something.

What you actually lost was interference.

Most of your stress never came from doing too much. It came from being interrupted too often, from managing reactions, from responding to messages that did not matter, and from maintaining emotional availability for people who were not aligned with your direction.

Noise kept you busy. Quiet lets you build.

A quiet life is not empty but intentional. It is not lonely but focused. It is not boring but disciplined.

People romanticize chaos because chaos creates the illusion of importance. If everything feels urgent, you feel needed; if everyone is calling you, you feel relevant; and if you are constantly reacting, you feel alive.

But relevance without direction is a trap.

When you choose clarity over access, people fall away. Conversations shorten, social obligations disappear, invitations slow down, and some relationships fade. That is not punishment. That is alignment correcting itself.

Your life gets quieter because fewer people have access to you. And that access reduction is exactly what creates peace. You start hearing your own thoughts again, noticing what actually matters, and feeling your body relax.

That quiet is not absence. It is presence.

You will notice how much of your energy was tied up in unnecessary interaction, how much of your time was spent explaining choices that did not need explanation, and how much of your emotional capacity was being used to regulate other people. Quiet gives all of that back to you.

The reason quiet feels uncomfortable at first is that it exposes how little time you spend with yourself. You were distracted. Entertained. Engaged. Busy. Quiet removes distraction and forces you to sit with your own thoughts.

That is where growth happens.

People who cannot tolerate quiet usually cannot tolerate themselves. They need noise to avoid reflection, constant input to avoid accountability, and stimulation to avoid stillness. You do not.

A quiet life allows consistency, routines, depth, and momentum that is not constantly reset by outside influence.

You stop reacting and start responding, stop consuming and start creating, and stop explaining and start executing.

Quiet makes all of that possible.

You might feel guilt when your life gets quieter, feel like you are neglecting people, or feel like you should reach out more. That guilt is leftover conditioning telling you that availability equals worth. It does not.

Your worth is not measured by how many people have access to you. It is measured by how aligned you are with your own life.

Some people will interpret your quiet as distance, others will interpret it as arrogance, and a few will say you disappeared. Let them say it. You did not disappear. You arrived.

The right people do not need constant access to feel connected. They understand seasons, respect focus, and do not demand explanations.

The wrong people need noise to maintain influence. They will try to pull you back into chaos, create urgency where none exists, and frame your quiet as a problem. Do not respond. Silence is not neglect when it is intentional, quiet is not abandonment when it is purposeful, and distance is not rejection when it is protective. Your life will get quieter as you get clearer. That is the natural order of things.

Do not fill the quiet with new noise, replace old chaos with new distractions, scroll your peace away, or invite confusion back in out of boredom. Protect the quiet.

In that quiet, you will build things that do not need applause, make decisions that do not require consensus, and move without being watched. That is power.

The loudest lives are rarely the most meaningful. Meaning grows in silence, consistency, and focus.

Quiet is not the end. It is the beginning.

Chapter 19

ACTION PLAN
FOR CHANGE

1. Identify one source of unnecessary noise in your life: conversations, social media, obligations, or constant availability.

2. Remove or reduce it for two weeks without announcing the change.

3. Use the quiet intentionally to think, plan, read, build, and rest.

4. Notice how your stress levels and focus shift without constant input.

5. Commit to protecting at least one daily window of quiet moving forward.

Quiet is not emptiness. It is space for your life to finally take shape.

AUTHORITY IS RETURNING TO WHERE IT ALWAYS BELONGED — YOU.

FXCK THEM is how you finally live

This is not a slogan. It is not a phase. It is not something you say when you are angry and forget when things calm down. FXCK THEM is how you finally live when you stop negotiating with your own life.

Up until now, you have been practicing. Testing boundaries. Pulling back. Letting go. Getting quieter. Choosing yourself again and again. This chapter is not about learning something new. It is about locking it in.

Living FXCK THEM means you stop treating your life like a group decision.

It means you wake up and move based on alignment, not approval, make choices without rehearsing explanations, and accept that not everyone will understand and you no longer need them to.

You already know what this feels like now: the calm, the clarity, the absence of chaos, and the steadiness. That is not luck. That is the result of authority returning to where it always belonged.

You.

FXCK THEM is what happens when you stop abandoning yourself under pressure, stop explaining your boundaries into weakness, and stop seeking permission from people who are not building your future.

This is where people get it twisted. They think FXCK THEM means aggression, isolation, anger, burning bridges, and cutting everyone off. It does not.

It means discernment.

It means you stop giving equal weight to unequal voices, stop letting convenience masquerade as love, and stop confusing noise with connection.

Living this way is quiet. Boring to outsiders. Unimpressive on the surface. And powerful beyond measure.

You no longer need to announce growth, defend choices, or explain silence.

You move.

People will still talk. They always do. The difference now is it does not reach you. Their opinions hit the wall of your clarity and fall flat. You are no longer porous. You are solid.

That solidity changes everything.

You stop reacting emotionally, oscillating between confidence and doubt, and asking if you are wrong for choosing yourself.

You know the biggest shift is internal. You trust yourself again. Not because you became perfect but because you stopped betraying your instincts, stopped overriding your inner voice to keep peace, and stopped outsourcing decisions to people who do not live with the consequences.

That trust is freedom.

You will still feel fear. Courage is not the absence of fear. It is action without negotiation. You will still disappoint people, which is unavoidable. You will still be misunderstood, which is normal. You will still lose relationships, which is necessary.

What you will not lose anymore is yourself.

Living FXCK THEM means you stop revisiting decisions to soothe others, stop reopening doors you already closed, stop apologizing for clarity, and stop explaining growth like it is a crime.

You accept that some people will never like the version of you that no longer needs them.

That acceptance is peace.

This book does not end with a hug. It ends with responsibility. Nobody is coming to hold you accountable. Nobody is going to enforce your boundaries for you. Nobody is going to protect your time if you do not.

This is where excuses end.

You know what drains you, what delays you, and what you need to let go of.

If you go back to old patterns after reading this, that is a choice, not confusion, not habit, and not circumstance.

A choice.

FXCK THEM is choosing alignment even when it costs you, choosing direction over comfort, and choosing your life without apology.

Not once. Not when it is easy. But consistently.

You do not need another book after this. You need action.

Close this book and live it.

Chapter 20

ACTION PLAN FOR CHANGE

1. Write down the one area of your life where you still hesitate to fully choose yourself.

2. Identify the person group or expectation you are still negotiating with.

3. Decide today what alignment looks like in that area without compromise.

4. Take one irreversible step within the next seventy-two hours. Something that makes going back uncomfortable.

5. Commit to living FXCK THEM daily through action, not words: boundaries, consistency, and movement.

This is not the end of the work. This is the start of your life.

STAYING IS STILL A DECISION, AND IT ALWAYS COSTS YOU TOMORROW.

Comfort is the most expensive drug you'll ever take

Nobody warns you that comfort will rob you quietly. Not all at once. Not dramatically. Not in a way that forces change. It steals from you slowly, through routines that feel safe and choices that feel reasonable.

Comfort does not feel like danger. It feels like relief.

It feels like staying where you are because at least you know what to expect. It feels like tolerating situations that drain you because the alternative feels uncertain. It feels like saying, "It's not that bad," while your life keeps getting smaller. Comfort is not peace. It is sedation.

You are not stuck because you are incapable. You are stuck because you are emotionally addicted to familiar pain. You know how to survive where you are. You know how to cope. You know how to manage disappointment, frustration, and exhaustion because you have been doing it for years. What you do not know is who you become when you stop settling. And that unknown scares you more than your current misery. So you stay.

You stay in relationships that no longer respect you because loneliness feels louder than disrespect.

You stay in jobs that drain your confidence because instability feels scarier than being undervalued.

You stay in habits that keep you small because discipline feels like pressure, and pressure feels risky.

Comfort convinces you that survival is enough.

It tells you to be grateful. It tells you not to complain.

It tells you that other people have it worse. It tells you that wanting more means you are unappreciative.

You listen because comfort always sounds reasonable.

But comfort never asks if you are fulfilled.

Comfort never asks if you are growing. Comfort never asks if you are becoming who you are capable of being. Comfort only asks if you can tolerate today. And if you keep answering yes, your future keeps shrinking.

You keep calling it timing. It is comfort. You keep calling it patience. It is comfort. You keep calling it being realistic. It is comfort.

Real change never feels realistic at first. It feels reckless. It feels disruptive. It feels like you are risking everything, even when you are really just risking familiarity.

Your nervous system prefers what it knows, even when that knowledge is harmful. That is why people return to the same situations, the same relationships, the same cycles over and over again. Not because they are stupid. Because their body confuses familiarity with safety.

So when opportunity shows up, it feels threatening.

When growth shows up, it feels uncomfortable. When change shows up, it feels wrong.

Comfort steps in and says, "Let's not do anything drastic." Drastic is usually where freedom starts.

Comfort is expensive because you do not pay for it with money. You pay for it with years. You pay for it with delayed dreams. You pay for it with unused potential. You pay for it with quiet resentment that builds until you barely recognize yourself.

One day, you wake up and realize you have been surviving for a long time, but you have not been living.

Comfort also lies to you about consequences. It tells you that staying is neutral, that waiting costs nothing, and that doing nothing is safer than doing something. But staying is still a choice, and every choice has a price.

The price of comfort is always tomorrow.

Tomorrow I'll start.

Tomorrow I'll leave.

Tomorrow I'll change.

Tomorrow I'll take myself seriously.

Tomorrow becomes years.

Comfort does not destroy your life in obvious ways. It just delays it until it is almost too late to start.

And the worst part is that nobody will tell you to move.

People will adapt to the version of you that stays.

They will build expectations around your consistency.

They will benefit from your availability, your tolerance, and your patience.

And when you finally think about changing, comfort will whisper, "Look how many people rely on you. Look how much you would disrupt."

That is how comfort traps you inside responsibility that was never supposed to be a prison.

You are allowed to want more than tolerable.

You are allowed to want more than manageable.

You are allowed to want a life that does not require constant coping.

Growth will feel chaotic at first.

It will disrupt routines. It will create temporary instability. It will force you to face parts of yourself you have been avoiding. But instability is not destruction. It is reorganization. Everything that expands must first stretch. And stretching hurts before it strengthens.

Comfort keeps you small because small feels controllable.

But you were not built for control. You were built for capacity. Every time you choose comfort over courage, you reinforce the belief that you cannot handle more. And that belief becomes identity.

You start to see yourself as someone who settles.

Someone who waits. Someone who plays it safe. And then you wonder why life never opens up.

Life opens up when you show that you are willing to move even when you are afraid.

Comfort is not your friend. It is your longest relationship. And it is the one that has cost you the most.

Chapter 21

ACTION PLAN FOR CHANGE

1. Identify one area of your life where you are staying only because it feels familiar, not because it is fulfilling. Write it down without justifying it. Familiarity doesn't mean it's right—it just means it's known.

2. Ask yourself what you are really afraid of losing if you change. Be honest, not dramatic. Be precise. You're not afraid of change—you're afraid of what dissolves when you change.

3. Decide on one uncomfortable action you can take in the next 72 hours that moves you out of comfort and into growth. Uncomfortable is the signal you're on the edge of growth.

4. Do not wait to feel ready. Move while you are unsure. Readiness follows action, not the other way around. Waiting to feel ready keeps you anchored to the familiar. Action disrupts the loop.

5. Remind yourself daily: discomfort is not danger. It is an expansion. Repeat daily: Discomfort is not harm. It's growth in motion.

Comfort will always invite you to stay.

Your future is asking you to move.

Choose which voice you are going to listen to.

YOUR FUTURE IS BUILT BY WHAT YOU DO WHEN YOU DON'T FEEL LIKE IT.

Discipline is real.

Discipline Is Louder Than Motivation

Motivation shows up when you feel inspired, when the mood is right, when the energy is high, when you are excited about what could happen. Discipline shows up when none of that is present, and you still move anyway.

That is the difference.

Most people keep waiting to feel ready. They wait for confidence. They wait for clarity. They wait for the right emotional state. And while they wait, their lives stay exactly the same.

Discipline does not wait for feelings. It moves first and lets feelings catch up.

You keep saying you want change, but your daily behavior says you want comfort more. Not because you are lazy, but because you built a life that runs on emotional permission.

If you feel like it, you do it. If you don't, you postpone. That pattern does not build futures. It builds excuses.

Your life looks the way it does because of what you repeatedly do, not what you repeatedly think about.

You cannot think your way into a different reality. You have to behave your way into it.

Discipline is not about being extreme. It is about being consistent. Small actions done daily beat big plans never done. Discipline feels hard is because it forces you to confront how much control your impulses actually have over you.

Right now, your comfort decides when you work.

Your mood decides when you try.

Your energy decides when you commit.

That means your future is being negotiated by how you feel.

And feelings are unreliable.

Discipline is about stopping your emotions from running your life.

It is choosing structure over spontaneity.

Standards over excuses.

Commitment over convenience.

And yes, that feels boring. That is why it works.

People romanticize hustle and grind, but real progress is repetitive. It is unsexy. It is doing the same right thing even when nobody is watching, and nothing exciting is happening yet.

That is the part most people quit.

They want results without routines.

Success without sacrifice.

Confidence without evidence.

But confidence is built through proof. Proof comes from keeping promises to yourself. And every time you break a promise to yourself, your mind remembers.

That is why you doubt yourself now.

Not because you are incapable.

Because you trained yourself not to trust your own word.

You told yourself you would start. You didn't.

You told yourself you would stop. You didn't.

You told yourself you would change. You waited.

Your brain keeps score.

Discipline rebuilds self-trust. Every time you do what you said you would do, you collect proof that you are reliable. And that proof changes how you see yourself.

Identity follows behavior.

You do not become disciplined by believing in yourself. You believe in yourself because you become disciplined.

Motivation tries to hype you. Discipline trains you.

And training is what lasts when emotions fade.

You also need to understand that discipline is not about punishment. It is about alignment. It is about choosing habits that align with the life you say you want, rather than the one you are currently tolerating.

If you say you want more, your schedule has to reflect that.

If you say you want growth, your routines have to support that.

If you say you want change, your behavior has to prove that.

If it does not, then your desire is just a fantasy.

Fantasy feels good. Discipline feels heavy. But fantasy does nothing for your future.

Discipline also protects you from burnout. When everything depends on bursts of motivation, you either overdo it or do nothing. You swing between extremes. Discipline creates rhythm. Rhythm creates sustainability.

You do not need to go harder. You need to go steadier.

Most people quit not because they are weak, but because they build lives that are impossible to maintain. They start too fast, with no structure, no plan, no realistic systems. Then, when life happens, everything collapses.

Discipline builds systems that work even when life gets messy.

You stop relying on willpower.

You stop negotiating with yourself.

You stop making every decision emotional.

You create defaults.

This is what I do.

This is who I am.

This is what happens even when I'm tired.

That is how real change sticks.

Discipline also means you stop romanticizing your potential and start respecting your process. Potential means nothing if you do not activate it. Everyone has potential. Few have discipline.

That is why talent does not win. Systems do.

You have been waiting to feel different before acting differently. That is backwards. You act differently until you become different.

Nobody wakes up one day magically disciplined. They become disciplined by repeatedly choosing discomfort over excuses.

And yes, at first it feels forced.

It feels unnatural.

It feels like you are pretending to be someone you are not.

That is because you are.

You are practicing being the person you are becoming.

Discipline is identity training.

Eventually, what felt forced becomes automatic.

But you have to survive the beginning.

You also need to stop pretending that discipline means perfection. You will miss days. You will mess up. You will fall off. The difference is that disciplined people do not quit in the face of setbacks. They resume.

They do not turn one bad day into a bad month.

They do not let guilt turn into paralysis.

They do not let mistakes become identity.

They correct and continue.

That ability to continue is what separates people who change from people who talk.

Discipline is not dramatic. It is quiet. It is private. It does not look impressive online. But it builds everything you want.

You want confidence? Discipline.

You want momentum? Discipline.

You want stability? Discipline.

You want freedom? Discipline.

Freedom is not doing whatever you want.

Freedom is having control over yourself.

And right now, if we are being honest, your impulses have more control over you than your goals do.

That can change.

But not through hype.

Through habits.

Through showing up when you don't feel like it.

Through doing the work even when nobody is clapping.

Through choosing long-term outcomes over short-term relief.

That is the work.

It is not glamorous.

But it is powerful.

Chapter 22

ACTION PLAN FOR CHANGE

1. Choose one daily habit that directly supports the life you say you want. Not ten. One. Pick the habit that says, "I'm serious about this."

2. Decide on a fixed time when that habit happens every day, regardless of mood. You don't decide whether to do it—only how you show up that day.

3. Track it for fourteen days. Do not aim for perfection. Aim for consistency. Tracking isn't about judgment. It's about visibility.

4. When you miss a day, do not quit. Resume immediately the next day without guilt. This is how habits become resilient instead of fragile.

5. After two weeks, add one more habit only if the first one feels stable. Expansion comes after stability—not before.

Stop waiting to feel motivated. Start building evidence that you can trust yourself. Discipline will not hype you. But it will change your life.

IF IT'S ON YOU, YOU DON'T HAVE TO WAIT ANYMORE.

Nobody is coming to save you

This is the moment most people avoid because it removes every excuse they have been hiding behind. Nobody is coming. No perfect opportunity. No flawless plan. No person can suddenly fix everything and make your life easier. Support can help. Advice can guide.

But rescue is not real. Waiting for rescue keeps you passive. Ownership makes you powerful.

As long as you believe someone else is responsible for changing your situation, you will stay exactly where you are. You will keep explaining why things are hard instead of deciding what to do about them.

You tell yourself you are waiting on timing.

You are waiting on courage.

You tell yourself you need more information.

You are avoiding responsibility.

You tell yourself you are healing first.

But you are also hiding.

Healing does not mean pausing your life indefinitely. It means learning how to move differently while you build strength. Pain explains behavior. It does not justify permanent paralysis.

At some point, you have to stop asking why this happened to you and start asking what you are going to do with what happened to you.

Your past shaped you. It does not get to decide your future forever.

Waiting feels responsible because it avoids risk. But nothing changes without risk. Waiting only feels safe because it protects you from immediate failure. It does nothing to protect you from long-term regret.

Regret is quiet at first. Then one day it gets loud.

You keep hoping for clarity before action. But clarity is built through action. You learn what works by trying. You learn what does not by failing. You learn who you are by making decisions, not by analyzing possibilities.

There is no version of your life where everything feels certain before you move. That is not how growth works. That is how comfort works.

Comfort says, "Stay."

Fear says, "Wait."

Growth says, "Move."

And growth does not care if you feel ready.

You also need to understand something uncomfortable. Some people prefer you to be dependent. Some systems benefit from you staying stuck. Some relationships only work when you are unsure and emotionally flexible.

When you take ownership, dynamics shift. People lose influence. Situations lose control. And that threatens anything that relied on your hesitation.

So do not expect applause when you finally decide to take your life seriously. Do not expect instant support. Do not expect everyone to understand. Expect resistance. Expect doubt. Expect pushback. That is normal when you stop playing the role people got comfortable with.

But resistance does not mean you are wrong. It usually means you are no longer convenient. Ownership means you stop outsourcing your future to circumstances, people, luck, timing, or trauma. It means you accept that what happens next is on you. Not in a harsh way. In a powerful way. Because if it is on you, then you can change it.

You have more control than you want to admit, and that truth is uncomfortable because it removes the story that keeps you safe from responsibility.

Victim stories protect your ego. Ownership builds your life. And yes, ownership is scary. It means if things do not work, you cannot blame the situation anymore. It means you have to face your own decisions. But it also means you get credit for your progress.

You are not powerless. You are just undecided. You have been waiting for permission to choose yourself. Permission is not coming. You have been waiting for someone to see your potential and invest in you. You have to invest in yourself first.

You have been waiting for confidence to arrive before you act. Confidence is built by acting. Everything you want is on the other side of responsibility. Not perfect responsibility.

Not knowing everything. Just choosing to stop waiting. Waiting keeps you safe. Ownership makes you free. You do not need to know the whole path. You need to take the next step.

One phone call. One application. One conversation. One routine change. One boundary.

Small steps done consistently beat perfect plans that never leave your head. You do not need a miracle. You need momentum. Momentum does not come from thinking. It comes from moving.

And yes, you might fail. Yes, you might choose wrong sometimes. Yes, you might feel embarrassed. Yes, you might have to restart. So what. Failure does not destroy you. Staying stuck does.

You have already survived worse than trying and missing. What you have not survived yet is living with the knowledge that you never tried at all.

Nobody is coming to save you, and that is not bad news. It is freedom. It means you do not have to wait anymore. It means you do not have to be chosen. It means you do not have to prove yourself to anyone before you start.

You can decide. Today.

Chapter 23

ACTION PLAN FOR CHANGE

1. Write down one problem in your life you keep explaining instead of changing. Explanation can feel productive, but here it's become containment. Write the problem down plainly, without backstory.

2. Ask yourself what part of this situation is actually within your control. Focus only on that. Control is smaller than you want—but more powerful than you think.

3. Choose one action you can take this week that moves the situation forward, even slightly. Even a 5% shift breaks stagnation. Forward motion matters more than scale.

4. Do not announce it. Do not debate it. Just do it. Action taken quietly builds internal authority— the kind that doesn't need witnesses.

5. Repeat this process weekly until your identity shifts from waiting to acting. Each week, repeat: Name → Control → Action → Silence.

Nobody is coming. So become the person you have been waiting for. You don't need better reasons. You need momentum.

YOU ARE NOT MEANT TO LIVE IN ONE CHAPTER OF YOUR OWN STORY.

Chapter 24

You will outgrow this version of yourself too

The version of you reading this book is not who you are going to be.

That matters more than you think.

Right now, you are fighting to become stronger, clearer, more disciplined, and more confident. You are trying to break patterns, set boundaries, and build a better life. That is necessary. But what nobody tells you is that one day, even this version of you will feel outdated.

If you get attached to who you are becoming right now, you will eventually become your own obstacle.

Growth does not stop once you finally get proud of yourself.

It keeps going.

You will outgrow habits that once saved you, goals that once felt impossible, identities that once felt powerful.

And if you refuse to release them, you will stall.

People think they get stuck because they fail. Most people get stuck because they succeed and then get comfortable with the version of themselves that worked.

You finally learn to say no, so you turn into someone who never says yes.

You finally build discipline, so you become rigid and stop adapting.

You finally get confidence, so you stop listening and stop growing.

Every stage of growth has blind spots.

The survival version of you needed protection.

The rebuilding version of you needs structure.

The expanding version of you will need flexibility.

If you keep using old strategies in new seasons, you will sabotage yourself while thinking you are staying consistent.

Consistency in values is powerful. Consistency in methods can become a limitation.

You are not meant to master one version of yourself and stay there. You are meant to keep evolving.

That means some of what you are learning now will eventually need to be unlearned. Some of your current rules will need to be rewritten. Some of your boundaries will need to shift. Some of your definitions of success will need to change. That will feel scary, because your brain loves stability.

Identity feels safe.

You start to say things like, "That's just how I am," and you use that sentence to protect yourself from growth. You turn personality into a cage.

You call it knowing yourself.

Sometimes it is just resisting change.

The strongest people are not the ones who lock into one identity. They are the ones who keep updating who they are as they become.

You cannot grow and stay loyal to every old version of yourself at the same time.

Some parts of you will need to die for new parts to live.

That does not mean you failed. It means you evolved.

The problem is that evolution costs certainty. It means stepping into spaces where you are no longer the expert. It means risking looking inexperienced again. It means admitting that what once worked may not work forever.

Ego hates that. Ego wants you to protect the image you finally built.

Growth wants you to keep learning. And the longer you protect an identity, the harder it becomes to expand beyond it. That is why people peak. That is why people plateau.

That is why people say, "This is just how I do things," even when it is no longer working.

You are not meant to live in one chapter of your own story. You are meant to turn pages.

This also applies to pain. Some of you are still living as if you are in survival mode, even though the danger is gone. You built defense mechanisms that once kept you safe, but now they keep you isolated.

You built emotional armor when you needed it. Now you might need a connection. You built hyper-independence despite having no support. Now you might need collaboration. You built emotional detachment when you were overwhelmed.

Now you might need vulnerability. But growth requires honesty about what season you are in.

You cannot heal while pretending you are still in crisis.

You cannot expand while acting like you are still surviving.

At some point, you have to stop letting old wounds define new decisions. Healing is not becoming unbreakable. Healing is becoming flexible. Strong enough to protect yourself. Open enough to receive more. That balance changes as you grow. If you cling to the old version of yourself because it feels powerful or familiar, you will eventually feel restless, bored, or blocked without knowing why. That feeling is not failure. It is your next level calling you forward.

Growth will keep asking you to let go of who you were so you can become who you are capable of being. Every time you resist, life will apply pressure until you move. You can evolve willingly, or you can be forced. Either way, change is coming. The choice is whether you grow with it or fight it.

Do not make loyalty to your past personality more important than your future potential.

You are allowed to reinvent yourself multiple times in one lifetime.

You are allowed to want different things as you grow.

You are allowed to change your definition of success.

You are allowed to update your boundaries, your priorities, and your identity.

You are not unstable for evolving. You are alive. And life does not stay still.

Chapter 24

ACTION PLAN FOR CHANGE

1. Identify one habit, belief, or role that once helped you but now limits you. What worked then isn't wrong—it's just outdated.

2. Ask yourself what it protected you from and whether that threat still exists. Then ask the second question—the one that matters now: *Does that threat still exist in the same way?*

3. Choose one small behavior shift that reflects the person you are becoming, not the one you were. Behavior updates identity faster than insight ever will.

4. Expect discomfort. Growth always feels unfamiliar at first. Your nervous system prefers what's known—even if it's limiting.

5. Repeat this process every few months so your identity evolves with your life. This is how growth stays integrated instead of chaotic.

Do not get attached to who you are today. Stay loyal to who you are becoming. You're not losing yourself. You're refining yourself.

PRESSURE DOESN'T BREAK YOU — IT BUILDS CAPACITY.

Pressure is proof you are leveling up

If your life feels heavier right now, that is not an accident.

Pressure shows up when something important is happening. You do not feel pressure when nothing is expected of you. You feel pressure when your decisions matter, when people rely on you, when your next move has consequences.

Pressure is not a punishment.

It is a signal.

A signal that you are no longer operating at the same level.

Most people interpret pressure as a sign that they are failing. They think that if life feels hard, they must be doing something wrong. So they retreat, they slow down, they go back to what feels familiar.

But comfort is not where growth happens.

Pressure is what builds capacity.

Every time your responsibilities increase, your skill set must expand. Every time your expectations rise, your discipline must rise with it. Every time your environment demands more from you, your mindset has to level up.

That stretch feels uncomfortable because you are not used to carrying this much yet.

Athletes do not grow in comfort.

Muscles do not grow easily.

Leadership does not grow in silence.

Pressure forces adaptation.

The reason you feel stressed is not that you are weak; it is because you are being asked to become more than you were before.

Instead of seeing that as a challenge, you are treating it like a threat.

Pressure also exposes where your systems are lacking. When life gets heavier, whatever was sloppy starts to break. Time management, boundaries, routines, and emotional regulation all of it gets tested.

Pressure does not create problems.

It reveals them.

And that is good news because you cannot fix what you cannot see.

But most people panic when flaws are exposed. They interpret exposure as failure rather than as feedback. So instead of adjusting, they retreat.

They say, "This is too much."

What they really mean is, "I haven't built the systems to support this level yet."

And that can be fixed.

Pressure also brings isolation. The higher you climb, the fewer people can relate to what you are carrying. Not everyone understands the decisions you have to make, the stress you sit with, or the responsibility you feel.

That loneliness does not mean you are alone. It means you are changing environments.

You are no longer in rooms where everyone is dealing with the same level of responsibility. And that shift can feel uncomfortable because you are used to being understood.

But growth does not always come with community. Sometimes it comes with solitude.

Sometimes the next level requires separation so you can focus, recalibrate, and strengthen without constant noise.

Pressure will also test your priorities. When everything feels urgent, you find out what actually matters. You cannot do everything. You cannot save everyone. You cannot carry every responsibility and still perform at a high level.

Pressure forces selection.

You have to decide what gets your energy and what does not. You have to say no more often. You have to protect your time more aggressively. You have to become more intentional.

And that can feel selfish if you are used to being available to everyone.

Another truth nobody talks about: pressure often shows up right before breakthroughs.

Right before momentum.

Right before visibility.

Right before a major change.

Your comfort zone resists expansion. It sends stress signals to try to pull you back. Your mind starts telling you that you are overwhelmed, that you cannot handle this, that you should slow down.

But most of the time, you are not overwhelmed by the work. You are overwhelmed by the adjustment.

You are learning how to operate at a higher level.

That takes time.

During that time, it feels chaotic.

But chaos is not collapse.

It is restructuring.

Pressure is the phase where your old habits no longer work, but your new systems are not fully built yet. You are in between versions of yourself.

That in-between space is uncomfortable, but it is also necessary.

Do not confuse transition with failure.

You also need to stop personalizing pressure as if it means something is wrong with you. Pressure is not proof that you are unqualified. It is proof that you are being challenged to grow into your next capacity.

Every new level requires a new discipline.

If you try to operate at a higher level while clinging to old habits, you will feel exhausted and scattered. Not because you cannot handle it, but because you have not yet upgraded your structure.

Pressure is not asking you to quit.

It is asking you to evolve.

And yes, sometimes pressure means you need support, not retreat. Support is not weakness. It is a strategy. Strong people know when to build teams, systems, and safeguards to sustain success.

Burnout happens when you try to carry growth alone without adjusting how you operate.

Pressure is also a test of self-belief. When things feel heavy, your old doubts come back. You start questioning your decisions. You start wondering if you deserve what you are building. You start thinking about easier paths.

That is normal.

But do not let temporary discomfort rewrite your vision.

If you quit every time it gets heavy, you will never know what you were capable of carrying.

Pressure is proof that you are in the arena, not on the sidelines.

And growth only happens in the arena.

Chapter 25

ACTION PLAN FOR CHANGE

1. Identify one area where pressure has increased recently: responsibility, expectations, workload, or decisions.

2. Ask yourself what skills or systems need to improve to support this level: time management, boundaries, delegation, or discipline.

3. Choose one structural change you can make this week to reduce chaos and increase control.

4. Stop interpreting stress as failure and start seeing it as a training signal.

5. Remind yourself daily: pressure is temporary, capacity is permanent.

Pressure does not mean you are breaking. It means you are being built.

YOUR NEXT CHAPTER IS NOT IN THIS BOOK.

IT'S IN YOUR ACTIONS.

Chapter 26

Stop reading.
Start moving.

If you are still waiting for the perfect moment, close this book now and come back in five years when nothing has changed. There is no perfect time. There is only now and later. And later is where dreams go to die quietly. You do not need more information. You do not need more motivation. You do not need another sign. You need movement.

Everything you say you want is on the other side of the decisions you keep postponing. Not because you are incapable, but because you are comfortable thinking instead of acting.

Thinking feels productive. Planning feels responsible. Talking feels like progress. But none of that changes your life. Action does.

Right now, the gap between who you are and who you want to be is not talent, resources, or opportunity. It is consistency. It is courage. It is a daily execution when nobody is clapping.

So here is the truth, with no softness left in it.

Nobody is coming.

Nobody is responsible but you.

Nobody owes you the future you want.

You build it, or you don't.

That is not cruel.

That is freedom.

Because if it is on you, you do not have to wait any longer.

The No-Excuses Manifesto

From this point forward:

- I will stop negotiating with my comfort.
- I will stop delaying hard decisions.
- I will stop blaming circumstances for choices I refuse to make.
- I will stop expecting confidence before action.
- I will stop tolerating what drains me.
- I will stop explaining myself to people who are not aligned with my future.

- I will stop abandoning myself to keep others comfortable.
- I will move even when I am unsure.
- I will act even when I am afraid.
- I will choose discipline over impulse.
- I will choose growth over familiarity.
- I will choose responsibility over resentment.

Not someday. Now. Because my life is not waiting on perfect conditions. It is waiting on my commitment.

The 30-Day No-Excuses Challenge

This is not about perfection. This is about proving to yourself that you can keep your word. For the next 30 days, these are your non-negotiables.

Daily Standards

Every day, no matter what:

1. **One Hard Thing.** Do one task you normally avoid. One call, one conversation, one workout, one uncomfortable decision. Do not overthink it. Just do it.

2. **One Growth Action.** Something that moves your future forward. Learning, applying, building, improving. Even small counts, if consistent.

3. **No Complaining Without Action.** If you catch yourself complaining, take one step immediately to fix the
   issue. No venting without movement.

4. **Daily Discipline Window.** At least 30 minutes of
   focused effort on your goals with no phone, no distractions, no multitasking.

5. **Sleep and Energy Respect.** You do not build a strong
   future with a destroyed body. Protect your rest so you
   can execute.

Weekly Focus

Each week has a theme:

Week 1: Structure

Fix your schedule. Create routines. Eliminate obvious distractions. Stop letting chaos run your day.

Week 2: Boundaries

Say no. Reduce access. Protect your time and energy. Stop
being available to everyone.

Week 3: Execution

Push harder on your goals. Apply, launch, start, commit. No
more preparation only.

Week 4: Ownership

Evaluate honestly. Adjust systems. Take responsibility for what worked and what didn't without excuses.

Rules of the Challenge

- You do not wait to feel like it.
- You do not quit because you miss a day.
- You do not start over. You continue.
- Miss a day? Resume immediately.
- No guilt. No drama. Just discipline.
- You are not proving anything to anyone else.
- You are rebuilding trust in yourself.

What Will Change If You Do This

- You will start to see yourself differently.
- You will trust your own word.
- You will stop romanticizing comfort.
- You will stop waiting for permission.
- You will gain momentum that does not depend on mood. And momentum changes everything. Once you know you can move without perfect conditions, fear loses its grip. Fear only controls people who wait. Movers build power.

STAND UP.
MAKE THE CALL.
SEND THE MESSAGE.
START THE HABIT.
END THE SITUATION.
CHOOSE YOURSELF.

You already know what needs to change

You already know what you have been avoiding. You already know what decision keeps showing up in your mind. That is not a coincidence. That is your life asking you to step up. So after this chapter;

Do not highlight.

Do not screenshot.

Do not send quotes.

Stand up.

Make the call.

Send the message.

Start the habit.

End the situation.

Choose yourself.

Because FXCK THEM was never about anger. It was about choosing your future even when it costs you comfort, approval, and familiarity.

It was about finally acting like your life matters.

And it does.

So stop reading.

Start moving.

Your next chapter is not in this book.

It is in your actions.

...

If you made it here, you already know this book was not gentle on purpose. It was not written to comfort you. It was written to interrupt you.

Everything you read was already inside you. This book did not give you courage but removed excuses. It did not motivate you, but stripped away the noise you were hiding behind. It did not teach you who to be, but reminded you who you stopped being to survive other people's expectations.

Now comes the part nobody can do for you.

There is no next chapter, no follow-up explanation, and no permission slip coming. There is only behavior.

If you close this book and go back to explaining yourself, nothing changes. If you close this book and keep negotiating your life, nothing changes. If you close this book and wait for the right time, nothing changes.

Insight without action is just entertainment.

You already know who drains you, what you have outgrown, and where you have been lying to yourself.

Do not disrespect what you now see by pretending you forgot it.

FXCK THEM only works if you live it quietly, consistently, and without apology. Not online, not in conversations, and not as a quote, but in decisions, in boundaries, in who you stop giving access to, and in what you finally choose.

Some people will never speak to you the same again, some doors will close permanently, and some versions of you will die.

That is not loss. That is alignment.

You do not need to announce anything, prove anything, or convince anyone. Just move.

The life you want does not require permission.

It requires honesty, discipline, and the courage to let people feel however they feel.

Close the book.

Go live like you meant every word.

About the Author

WALLO267 is proof that purpose has no borders. After serving twenty years behind bars, he turned his story into a global movement of resilience and reinvention. A *New York Times* bestselling author, cultural advisor at YouTube, former Chief Marketing Officer of Reform Alliance, and co-host of *Million Dollaz Worth of Game* (named by *The Hollywood Reporter* among the most powerful voices in podcasting, 2024), WALLO267 continues to merge impact and innovation. He uses partnerships, like his $4.5 million minority business initiative with Barstool Sports, his lifestyle brand ARPLNSNHOTLS, and his production company Nanny's House Entertainment, which develops and produces movies, TV series, books, and podcasts, to prove your past is data, not destiny.

Keep in Touch with Wallo267

Stay connected, stay inspired, and keep growing with me. I share daily messages, lessons, and moments to help you stay focused on becoming your best self.

Follow & connect on social:
Instagram • Facebook • TikTok • YouTube • X (Twitter)
@WALLO267

For speaking engagements, partnerships, and media inquiries:
✉ info@wallo267.co,
🌐 www.wallo267.co

Your journey matters.
Keep showing up for yourself every day.